HEALTHY Vegetarian COOKBOOK

Delicious and inspirational recipes for every occasion

Edited by JANE DONOVAN

APPLE

Published by Apple Press
Sheridan House
112-116A Western Road
Hove
East Sussex BN3 1DD

A QUINTET BOOK

Reprinted 2003
ISBN 1-84092-404-7

This book was designed and produced by
Quintet Publishing Limited
6 Blundell Street
London N7 9BH

Art Director: Clare Reynolds
Design: Siân Keogh
Project Editor: Doreen Palamartschuk
Editor: Jane Donovan
Illustrator: Shona Cameron

Creative Director: Richard Dewing
Publisher: Oliver Salzmann

Typeset in Great Britain by
Central Southern Typesetters, Eastbourne
Manufactured in China by
Regent Publishing Pte Ltd
Printed in China by
Leefung-Asco Printers Trading Limited

Material in this book previously appeared in:
Indian Vegetarian by Sumana Ray; *Chinese Vegetarian* by
Deh-Ta Hsiung; *Vegetarian Pizza* by Maureen Keller; *Fabulous Fruit*
by Moya Clarke; *Olio di Oliva* and *A Feast of Mushrooms* by
Marlena Spieler; *Southern Cooking, Salsa Cooking*, and
Cajun Cooking by Marjie Lambert; *Low-fat Vegetarian Cooking* by
Jenny Stacey; *The Pumpkin & Squash Cookbook* and *The Aubergine
Cookbook* by Rosemary Moon.

HEALTHY *Vegetarian* COOKBOOK

CONTENTS

INTRODUCTION

Today vegetarian food is no longer considered the preference of cranks—it is right where it should be: firmly established in the mainstream of everyday cooking and eating. Restaurants everywhere now offer vegetarian choices as part of their menus and many people are making a conscious decision to cut down on their intake of meat, especially red meat, and high-fat foods even if they do not completely change their eating habits. As we travel more widely and through newspaper and magazine articles, as well as television programmes, we are now better acquainted with the cuisine of other countries, where vegetarian cooking often features strongly. At the same time, a whole new range of ingredients is available in our supermarkets and food shops, and we can happily shop on a global scale in most towns and cities.

THE VEGETARIAN ISSUE

Throughout the world, the number of people who decide to follow the vegetarian way of eating is growing and in tropical climates (India, for example) where meat deteriorates extremely quickly, the native inhabitants grow their own vegetables and live off the land easily, so making themselves completely self-sufficient. More and more people find that they no longer enjoy the taste of meat or they may decide to cut down on the number of cholesterol-rich foods that they eat to reduce the risk of heart disease. On the other hand, many people are simply discovering how satisfying (and

economical) it is to produce a really delicious meal that contains absolutely no meat.

THE IMPORTANCE OF GOOD INGREDIENTS

To get the best results from any recipe, always buy the freshest ingredients and watch for seasonal produce in the shops. Local farmers often sell vegetables and fruits or you may even decide to grow your own. If you live in a flat, you could grow your own fresh herbs or plant tomatoes in window boxes or on the roof terrace. Also, only buy as much as you need; don't be tempted to buy in bulk or you will find that ingredients often lose their flavour, not to mention their natural goodness.

LOW FAT OR NO FAT?

Although it is recommended that fat intake be severely reduced, everything in moderation is your best maxim. Nobody is suggesting a totally fat-free diet. We all require a certain amount of fat for our bodies to function properly, to produce linoleic acid for skin maintenance, for growth in children, and for the supply of the necessary compounds. As we cannot produce these compounds ourselves, it is vital that we obtain them from food. Fat also enhances flavour. The following fat intake is recommended:

Less than ten per cent of our daily calories should come from saturated fats: up to ten per cent may come from polyunsaturated fats, and the remainder of our intake may come from

▲ *Fibre is an essential ingredient in a vegetarian diet*

monounsaturated sources. At present, many of us obtain at least 40 per cent of our total calorie intake from fat, so there is plenty of room for improvement in our diet.

Eating a low-fat diet (particularly a vegetarian diet) will improve your life and could increase your life expectancy. It has been proved that those who switch to a low-fat diet reduce their risk of heart disease and are also less susceptible to gallstones, diabetes, obesity, stomach upsets, thrombosis, eczema, asthma, arthritis and general lethargy. A low-fat and/or vegetarian diet will not only make you feel better and have more energy, it will also make you look better.

VEGETARIAN OR VEGAN?

Many people refer to themselves as vegetarians if they do not eat red meat, but this is inaccurate. A true vegetarian eats no animal flesh, which includes poultry and fish as well as red and white meat. Vegans, those who follow the strictest vegetarian diet, will not eat anything at all that is derived from

animals—no meat, fish, cheese, butter or any milk-based foods; indeed some also refuse honey, which they do not believe should be taken from the bees. A creative vegan diet is a great culinary challenge.

Lacto-vegetarians do not eat any foods that involve the slaughter of animals, so they will not eat eggs although they do include dairy products such as cheese and milk, whereas octo-lacto vegetarians will eat eggs.

There are growing numbers of would-be vegetarians, colloquially referred to as "demi-veg", who eat fish. This is especially true of those who are just beginning to turn to vegetarianism. This is a compromise in terms of true vegetarianism but one which many parents are happy to accept for their growing children.

FIBRE—THE KEY TO HEALTHY EATING

Fibre is the most important part of the vegetarian diet, the most effective weapon against the conditions brought on by the mediocrity of processed foods. Dietary fibre forms the cell walls of plants—the superstructure or skeleton. It is unique to plants and it is therefore easy to see that a diet rich in animal proteins and fat, but lacking in cereals and vegetables can be almost totally lacking in fibre.

Fibre is essential for the efficient working of the digestive system and therefore the processing of our food. A fibreless diet is easy to eat and presents little intestinal challenge. Indeed, much of the progress in the early days of the "food industry" was aimed at making eating "easier" by refining foods. Intestinal inactivity, however, can lead to a number of disorders and diseases. In the less

HOW TO LOWER YOUR FAT INTAKE

Talk is cheap. Action speaks louder than words. Now that you know the reasons why you should reduce your fat intake, here are some practical tips:

❖ Reduce the visible fats in your diet, such as those used in cooking and those eaten as snacks.

❖ Eliminate high-fat crisps, biscuits, fried foods, confectionery and processed foods. Substitute fat-free/low-fat crisps and fat-free biscuits.

❖ Reduce the amount of hard cheese you eat. Most of these cheeses contain 30–40 per cent fat in relation to their weight. Try using a little strong-flavoured cheese rather than a lot of mild cheese.

❖ Limit egg yolks to three a week, but continue to use egg whites as often as you like.

❖ Begin to discover the aroma and flavour of fresh herbs; these can enhance your cooking without piling on the calories.

❖ Avoid fried food. Try grilling or steaming. Alternatively, try poaching vegetables in a little liquid, with herbs and spices.

❖ Skim the fat off stews, casseroles and soups. You'll be surprised how much fat you can remove.

❖ Add more grains, pulses and beans to your diet. They are high in protein and fibre, and low in fat. If you are following a completely vegetarian diet, grains, pulses and beans will ensure a balanced diet and adequate protein.

❖ Pasta is filling, healthy and low in fat but watch what you use in your sauces!

❖ Switch to skimmed milk and you will hardly notice the difference in flavour. In recipes calling for cream, use full-cream milk or yoghurt.

❖ Substitute curd cheeses for cream cheeses.

developed countries of the world where the staple diet is rice, lentils and vegetables there is disease, but much of it is associated with vitamin deficiencies rather than a lack of dietary fibre.

To keep healthy it is important to cook with, and eat, as many unprocessed foods as possible, which leads inevitably to a high-fibre diet. What is amazing is that, even among meat-eaters, the foods that we think of as starches or carbohydrates (fibre foods) often contribute a significant amount of protein to the diet—between 20 and 30 per cent of the protein in an average diet comes from potatoes. Cut out the animal proteins, which automatically leads to a reduction in fat, increase fibre-rich foods and a healthy diet is easily achieved.

EXTRA PROTEINS FOR VEGETARIANS

Vegetable protein foods are becoming increasingly common, and there is quite a movement in agriculture towards soya, a high protein crop which can be used as solids or liquid and which produces a much better protein yield than livestock. This is

▲ *A balanced diet is essential for all vegetarians*

regarded as one of the more plausible ways of increasing the quality of the international diet.

Tofu, or bean curd, a relatively recent introduction to many Westerners but a staple protein food of the Chinese for many thousands of years, also has a valuable place in the vegetarian diet. Also known as soya bean curd, it is best when it is fresh and the texture is firm. Natural or smoked tofu may be sliced and quickly fried, then added to salads and other vegetable dishes, or beaten into fillings for pies and flans.

ROBUST FLAVOURS FOR ROBUST FOODS

Many beans and vegetables respond deliciously to a clever and inventive use of herbs and spices. Toasting your own whole spices, such as cumin and coriander seeds, in a dry saucepan and grinding them just before use achieves the best possible flavour. Alternatively, buy small quantities of ground spices and replace them regularly. Dried seasonings are only at their best for a few months and lose much of their flavour after a year.

Fresh herbs have the best flavour, but they can be very expensive, especially if you have to buy them from a supermarket. Keep freeze-dried herbs for emergencies but, if you are lucky enough to have a herb garden, try to use fresh herbs whenever possible. Herbs for garnish should be chopped and added at the last moment, to retain both colour and immediacy of flavour. Even if you do not have a garden it is a good idea to grow some herbs in pots on your windowsill—some varieties, such as basil, fare much better this way than grown outside in unreliable climates.

One of the most exciting trends in popular cooking in the last few years has been the use of salsas as salad garnishes, and these work especially well with bean-based dishes. A mixture as simple as an orange, tomatoes, spring onions, and toasted mustard seeds with fresh coriander and a chopped chilli can add the most exciting explosion of colour, texture, and flavour to a casserole or bake.

▲ *Fresh herbs add flavour and interest to many vegetarian dishes*

The recipes we have selected for the *Very Vegetarian Cookbook* prove just how varied and interesting a vegetarian diet can be. They may even inspire you to start experimenting with your own ideas. Whether you are a vegetarian already or just want some ideas for a healthier way of eating, you will find plenty of suggestions for every kind of meal including breakfasts and brunches, light suppers and lunches, and some classic vegetarian dishes. Happy cooking and eating!

BREAKFASTS AND BRUNCHES

APRICOT YOGHURT CRUNCH

Serves 4

*The combination of crunchy porridge oats, spicy yoghurt and lightly
poached fruit makes an attractive morning dish.*

INGREDIENTS

300 g/10 oz apricots, pitted

4 tbsp honey

175 g/6 oz porridge oats, toasted

¹/₂–1 tsp ground ginger

300 ml/¹/₂ pt plain yoghurt

Place the apricots in a saucepan with 150 ml/¹/₄ pt water and 1 tablespoon of the honey. Cook for 5 minutes until softened and drain. Mix the porridge oats and remaining honey in a bowl. Stir the ginger into the yoghurt. Alternately layer the fruit, yoghurt and porridge oat mixtures into serving glasses. Chill and serve.

PORRIDGE OATS WITH POACHED FRUIT

Serves 4

*A quick dish which can be made in advance or the night before. Hearty and
filling, the poached fruit sets off the porridge oats perfectly.*

INGREDIENTS

360 g/³/₄ lb porridge oats

1 litre/1³/₄ pt skimmed milk

*170 g/6 oz plums, halved, pitted and
sliced*

125 ml/4 fl oz honey

Place the porridge oats in a saucepan with the milk. Bring to the boil, reduce the heat and simmer for 5 minutes, stirring, until thickened.

Meanwhile, place the plums in a saucepan with 3 tablespoons of the honey and 150 ml/¹/₄ pt water. Bring to the boil, reduce the heat and simmer for 5 minutes until softened. Drain well.

Spoon the porridge into individual bowls and top with the poached plums. Serve piping hot and pour over the remaining honey, to taste.

◄ *Apricot Yoghurt Crunch*

CRUNCHY BREAKFAST BISCUITS

Makes 14

*These lightly spiced biscuits are delicious served piping hot with cinnamon yoghurt,
thus eliminating the need for butter.*

INGREDIENTS

180 g/6 oz self-raising flour

180 g/6 oz wholemeal self-raising flour

Pinch of ground cinnamon

Pinch of ground nutmeg

3 tbsp polyunsaturated margarine

50 g/2 oz All-bran cereal

1 tbsp chopped, skinned hazelnuts

3 tbsp raisins

1 egg

6 tbsp skimmed milk

For the cinnamon yoghurt

150 ml/¼ pt plain yoghurt

¼ tsp ground cinnamon

1 tsp honey

Preheat the oven to 200°C/400°F/Gas 6. Place the flours and spices in a bowl and rub in the margarine to resemble fine breadcrumbs. Stir in the All-bran, nuts and raisins. Stir in the egg and milk and bring together to form a soft dough.

Knead the dough on a lightly floured surface and cut into eight 7-cm/3-in rounds. Brush the tops with a little extra milk and place on a floured baking sheet. Bake for 20 minutes until risen and golden. Mix together the yoghurt ingredients and serve with the warm biscuits.

GRILLED PINK GRAPEFRUIT

Serves 4

A quick, simple breakfast dish; it is quick to prepare but its flavour is sensational.

INGREDIENTS

2 pink grapefruit

3 tbsp honey

Pinch of ground allspice

Mint sprigs, to garnish (optional)

Preheat the grill. Peel the grapefruit, remove the pith, and cut each grapefruit into quarters. Place the quarters in a heatproof shallow dish.

Mix together the honey and allspice and spoon over the grapefruit pieces. Cook under the grill for 5 minutes. Serve garnished with mint, if desired.

BREAKFAST HASH

Makes 4

*For a speedier breakfast, cook the potatoes for this tasty dish the evening before
and store in a sealed bag in the refrigerator until required.*

INGREDIENTS

375 g/12 oz peeled, cubed potatoes

1 tbsp sunflower oil

1 red pepper, halved and seeded

1 green pepper, halved and seeded

2 tomatoes, diced

*375 g/12 oz open cap mushrooms, peeled
and quartered*

4 tbsp chopped fresh parsley

Ground black pepper

Cook the potatoes in boiling water for 7 minutes, drain well. Heat the sunflower oil in a large frying pan, add the potatoes and cook for 10 minutes, stirring occasionally.

Chop the red and green peppers and add to the pan with the tomatoes and mushrooms. Cook for 5 minutes, stirring constantly. Add the chopped parsley, season to taste and serve.

FRUIT KEBABS

Serves 4

The perfect way to present fresh fruit, these lightly grilled kebabs, with a hint of mint, make a refreshing start to the day.

INGREDIENTS

3 tbsp fine granulated sugar

2 mint sprigs, plus extra to garnish

1 papaya, halved, seeded and chopped
into 5-cm/2-in squares

1 mango, pitted and chopped into
5-cm/2-in squares

1 star fruit, sliced

2 kiwi fruit, thickly sliced

Soak four wooden skewers in water for 30 minutes. Remove when ready to use. Place the sugar, mint and 150 ml/¼ pt water in a pan. Heat gently to dissolve the sugar and then bring to the boil until reduced by half. Discard the mint.

Thread the fruit onto the skewers, alternating the varieties. Brush with the syrup and grill for 10 minutes, turning and brushing until heated through. Serve hot, garnished with mint.

STRAWBERRY COCKTAIL

Serves 4

A refreshing breakfast cocktail with a sparkle. It is as quick and easy to make as it is to drink.

INGREDIENTS

225 g/8 oz strawberries, hulled and
chopped

200 ml/6 fl oz cranberry juice

3 tbsp honey

½ tsp ground ginger

600 ml/1 pt sparkling mineral water

Ice and mint sprigs, to serve

4 whole strawberries,
to garnish

Place the strawberries, cranberry juice, honey and ginger in a blender or food processor and blend for 30 seconds until smooth and creamy.

Add the sparkling mineral water, ice and mint. Pour into glasses, garnish with the strawberries and serve immediately.

HASH-BROWN POTATOES WITH BAKED BEANS

Serves 6

These golden potato cakes are served with a spicy bean dish, and are perfect for mopping up the delicious juices.

Make the bean dish in advance and refrigerate until morning.

Simply heat the beans in a pan over a gentle heat.

INGREDIENTS

For the baked beans

200 g/7 oz dried haricot beans, soaked overnight

150 ml/¼ pt vegetable stock

1 tsp dried mustard

1 onion, chopped

2 tbsp dark molasses

225 g/8 oz tomatoes, peeled, and chopped

1 tbsp tomato purée

1 tbsp chopped fresh basil

Ground black pepper

For the potato cakes

375 g/12 oz peeled, cubed potatoes

2 tbsp skimmed milk

1 onion, chopped

1 garlic clove, crushed

2 tsp sunflower oil

Drain the soaked beans and rinse well under cold water. Drain and put in a large saucepan with 500 ml/1 pint water. Bring the beans to the boil and boil rapidly for 10 minutes. Reduce the heat to a simmer, cover and cook for 1 hour or until the beans are cooked, topping up the water, if necessary. Drain the beans and return them to the pan. Stir in the vegetable stock, dried mustard, onion, molasses, tomatoes, tomato purée and basil. Season well and cook for 15 minutes or until the vegetables are cooked.

Meanwhile, make the potato cakes. Cook the potatoes in boiling water for 20 minutes or until just soft. Drain well and mash with the milk.

Add the onion and garlic, mixing well, and form into 12 equal-sized cakes. Brush a non-stick frying pan with the sunflower oil and warm over a medium heat. Cook the potato cakes for 15 to 20 minutes, turning once, until golden brown. Serve piping hot with the baked beans.

BREAKFAST CRUNCH

Serves 4–6

A delicious breakfast in a bowl, packed with goodness.

INGREDIENTS

30 g/1 oz sunflower seeds

30 g/1 oz pine nuts

30 g/1 oz sesame seeds

2 oranges

2 Tbsp brown sugar

75 g/3 oz dried figs, chopped

2 large bananas

500 g/1 pt Greek yogurt

Using a dry pan, roast the sunflower seeds and pine nuts for 3 minutes over medium heat, then add the sesame seeds and roast for a further 3 minutes, stirring to give even browning. Remove the pan from the heat.

Coarsely grate the peel from 1 orange and add to the pan with the sugar and dried figs. Stir until well combined and cook for 2 minutes. Leave to cool.

Remove the peel and pits from the oranges and cut them into pieces. Slice the bananas and mix with the oranges and yogurt, divide among four dishes and top each with the fig and seeds mixture. Serve at once.

BREAD PUDDING

Serves 8

*Renowned as a delicious dish, this savoury bread pudding is the perfect example
of adapting a recipe to low-fat without compromising on taste.*

INGREDIENTS

*6 slices wholemeal bread, with
crusts removed*

1 Tbsp polyunsaturated margarine

1 red pepper, halved and seeded

1 green pepper, halved and seeded

2 tomatoes, chopped

50 g/2oz low-fat Cheddar cheese, grated

2 egg whites, beaten

475 ml/16 fl oz skimmed milk

Ground black pepper

Spread the bread with the margarine and cut each slice into four triangles by cutting on the diagonal.

Place the peppers skin side uppermost on a rack and grill for 10 minutes until slightly blackened. Place in a plastic bag with tongs, seal and let cool. Peel off the skins and discard. Slice the peppers into thin strips.

Layer the bread, peppers, tomatoes and half of the cheese in a large shallow ovenproof dish. Mix the egg white and milk together and pour over the bread. Allow to stand for 30 minutes.

Sprinkle the remaining cheese over the dish and season. Cook in the oven at 170°C/325°F/Gas 3 for 45 minutes until set and risen. Serve hot.

APPLE DROP SCONES

Serves 4

This healthy version of a breakfast favourite is filled with chunks of crisp apple which are complemented by the cinnamon spiced yoghurt sauce.

INGREDIENTS

For the scones		For the yoghurt sauce
50 g/2oz wholemeal flour	85 ml/2 ½ fl oz skimmed milk	150 ml/1 ¼ pts low-fat natural yoghurt
1 tsp baking powder	1 green dessert apple, cored and chopped	½ tsp ground cinnamon
1 tsp caster sugar	1 Tbsp raisins	1 tsp honey
1 medium egg, beaten	Vegetable oil	

Sift the flour and baking powder for the scones into a mixing bowl and stir in the sugar. Make a well in the centre and beat in the egg and milk to make a smooth batter. Stir in the apple and raisins, mixing well.

Brush a heavy based frying pan with a little oil and warm over medium heat. Divide the batter into eight equal portions and drop four portions into the pan, spacing them well apart. Cook for 2 to 3 minutes until the top of each drop scone begins to bubble. Turn the scones over and cook for 1 minute. Transfer to a warmed plate while cooking the remaining scones.

Mix the yoghurt sauce ingredients together in a bowl. Serve with the hot drop scones.

BANANA ENERGY

Serves 4

If you can't face a full breakfast in the morning, take your energy in a glass with this nutritious drink.

INGREDIENTS

4 large bananas, peeled and cut into chunks

1 Tbsp lemon juice

300 ml/½ pt low-fat natural yoghurt

300 ml/½ pt skimmed milk

2 Tbsp honey

Lemon slices and mint sprigs, to garnish

Place all the ingredients in a food processor or blender. Blend for 1 minute until smooth and creamy. Pour into tall serving glasses, garnish with the lemon and mint, and serve immediately.

Apple Drop Scones ▶

SPICED PEARS

Serves 4

The aroma from this dish is almost as good as the taste, and all part of the enjoyment.
If liked, serve with a spoonful of natural yoghurt or cottage cheese.

INGREDIENTS

4 large ripe pears, peeled, halved,
and cored

300 ml/¹/₂ pt mango juice

1 cinnamon stick, crushed

¹/₂ tsp grated nutmeg

3 Tbsp raisins

2 Tbsp soft brown sugar

Place the pear halves in a pan with the fruit juice, spices, raisins and sugar. Heat gently to dissolve the sugar and then bring to the boil.

Reduce the heat to a simmer and cook for a further 10 minutes until the pears are softened. Serve hot with the syrup.

SPICY FRUIT SALAD

Serves 4

Dried fruits are filled with goodness and have a delicious, concentrated flavour of their own. With many varieties
now available it is easy to mix delicious combinations to create your personal favourite fruit salad.

INGREDIENTS

115 g/4 oz dried apricots

50 g/2 oz dried peaches

50 g/2 oz dried mango

50 g/2 oz dried pears

115 g/4 oz dried stoned prunes

1 tsp ground cinnamon

900 ml/1¹/₂ pts orange juice

3 mint sprigs

150 ml/¹/₄ pt) low-fat natural yoghurt

Grated zest of 1 orange

Place the fruits in a bowl and add the cinnamon and orange juice. Cover and leave to soak overnight.

Place the contents of the bowl in a saucepan with the mint and bring to the boil, reduce the heat to a simmer and

cook for 20 minutes until the fruits have softened. Cool and transfer to the refrigerator. Cover until required.

Remove the mint from the salad. Mix together the yoghurt and orange zest. Serve with the fruit salad.

Spiced Pears ▶

APPETIZERS AND SOUPS

STAR FRUIT AND ROCKET SALAD WITH RASPBERRY VINEGAR DRESSING

Serves 4

This makes a very good side salad or appetizer. Rocket has a strong, very distinctive flavour which is excellent when balanced with sweet salad leaves such as iceberg or Romaine lettuce, but do not be tempted to add too much rocket or cut it too coarsely as it will overpower the other delicate ingredients, especially the star fruit. If rocket is unavailable, one or two bunches of watercress may be used instead.

INGREDIENTS

½ iceberg lettuce, shredded

12 medium rocket leaves, finely shredded

3 spring onions, chopped

2 star fruit, sliced and quartered

For the dressing

3 tbsp raspberry vinegar

1 tsp caster sugar

Salt and ground black pepper

8 tbsp olive oil

Toss the lettuce, rocket and spring onions together in a salad bowl. Next make the dressing: place the vinegar in a bowl and whisk in the caster sugar with plenty of seasoning. Continue whisking until the sugar and salt have dissolved. Slowly add the olive oil, whisking all the time to combine the ingredients well.

Add the star fruit to the salad. Pour the dressing over and mix lightly. Serve at once. Do not leave the star fruit to stand for any length of time once it is cut as it dries on the surface and tends to discolour slightly around the edges.

PITTA OR NAAN BREAD WITH FETA SPREAD AND DUKKAH

Serves 4

Bread and olive oil, with a tangy mound of feta-yoghurt spread, and a sprinkling of the spiced Middle-Eastern nut mixture called dukkah, *is the classic breakfast throughout the Middle East. It also makes a great mid-afternoon snack.*

INGREDIENTS

3 garlic cloves, chopped

125–175 g/4–6 oz feta cheese, crumbled

3–4 tbsp yoghurt

Extra-virgin olive oil, as needed

$\frac{1}{2}$–1 tsp each: ground coriander, cumin and thyme

2–3 tbsp each: coarsely ground, toasted sesame seeds, and hazelnuts or almonds

To garnish

10–15 black olives, or as many as you like

3–5 spring onions

4–8 warm pitta breads or 2–4 warm naan breads, torn into pieces and wrapped in a cloth

Combine the chopped garlic with the crumbled feta, yoghurt and 1 to 2 tablespoons of olive oil. Mound onto a plate. Combine the coriander, cumin, thyme, sesame seeds and nuts to make *dukkah*. Pour a few tablespoons of olive oil onto a saucer and sprinkle with the *dukkah* mixture. Garnish with the olives and spring onions.

Serve the plate of cheese mixture and the olive oil–spice platter with the pitta or naan bread. Let each person dip into the various mixtures as desired, combining to taste.

ASPARAGUS WITH RED PEPPER SAUCE

Serves 4

This bright red pepper sauce looks terrific spooned over asparagus spears. If you don't want to make a spicy sauce, either reduce the amount of chilli sauce, or omit it altogether.

INGREDIENTS

For the sauce	Juice of 1 lemon
3 red peppers, halved and seeded	1 garlic clove, crushed
600 ml/1 pt vegetable stock	500 g/1 lb asparagus spears, trimmed
1 tsp chilli sauce	Grated rind of 1 lemon
	Parsley sprigs, to garnish

To make the sauce, cook the peppers under a hot grill, skin side uppermost, for 5 minutes until the skin begins to blacken and blister. Transfer the peppers to a polythene bag using tongs, seal and leave for 20 minutes. Peel the skin from the peppers and discard.

Roughly chop the peppers and put them in a saucepan with the stock, chilli sauce, lemon juice and garlic.

Cook over a gentle heat for 20 minutes or until the peppers are tender. Transfer the sauce to a blender and blend for 10 seconds. Return the purée to the saucepan and heat through gently.

Meanwhile, tie the asparagus spears into four even bundles. Stand upright in a steamer or saucepan filled with boiling water and cook for 10 to 15 minutes until tender. Remove the asparagus from the pan and untie the bundles. Arrange on four serving plates and spoon the sauce over the top. Sprinkle the lemon rind over the top, garnish with parsley and serve.

MEDITERRANEAN TOASTS

Serves 4

These bite-sized hot open sandwiches are delicious as a snack. Use eight slices of a French stick if preferred. For the best flavour be sure to cook these just before serving.

INGREDIENTS

4 large, thick slices of ciabatta or other crusty bread	*4 ripe tomatoes, peeled and chopped*
2 garlic cloves, crushed	*1 tbsp tomato purée*
1 tbsp low-fat polyunsaturated spread, melted	*4 black olives, pitted and chopped*
	Ground black pepper
	Basil leaves, to garnish

Toast the bread under the grill for 2 minutes each side. Mix the garlic and melted low-fat spread together and drizzle onto one side of the toasted bread.

Mix the tomatoes, tomato purée and olives together, season and spoon onto the toast. Cook under the grill for 2 to 3 minutes or until hot. Remove the toasts from under the grill and cut in half. Garnish with basil leaves and serve.

BAKED POTATO SKINS

Serves 4

Always a firm favourite, the potato skins should be prepared a day in advance for ease and speed.
Pop them in the oven to warm them through before serving.

INGREDIENTS

4 medium baking potatoes

For the yoghurt dip

150 ml/¼ pt plain yoghurt

2 garlic cloves, crushed

1 tbsp chopped spring onions

For the mustard sauce

150 ml/¼ pt plain yoghurt

2 tsp wholegrain mustard

1 jalapeño chilli, chopped

For the tomato salsa

2 medium tomatoes, chopped

3 tbsp finely chopped red onion

1 tbsp chopped fresh parsley

1 green pepper, seeded and chopped

Pinch of sugar

Scrub the potatoes and place on a baking sheet. Bake at 200°C/400°F/Gas 6 for 1 hour or until soft. Remove and cool. Cut the potatoes in half lengthwise and scoop out the centres with a teaspoon, leaving a 1-cm/½-in thick shell. Sprinkle the skins with salt and place the potatoes in the oven for 10 minutes or until crisp.

Mix the yoghurt dip ingredients together. Mix together the mustard sauce ingredients. Finally mix the tomato salsa ingredients together. Place each dip in a separate bowl and cover until required. Serve the hot potato wedges with the dips.

TOMATO-BASIL SOUP WITH RED PEPPER SALSA

Serves 4

This is a delightful hot-weather soup, perfect for late summer when the garden is producing an abundance of tomatoes. Use the best tomatoes you can find, since this recipe relies on the lush flavour of ripe tomatoes. The soup should be made early in the day and chilled until serving time.

INGREDIENTS

2 garlic cloves, crushed	*3 tbsp extra-virgin olive oil*	*1 tbsp balsamic vinegar*
5 tbsp chopped fresh basil	*1.8 kg/4 lb ripe tomatoes*	*½ tsp salt*
¼ tsp ground black pepper	*225 ml/8 fl oz chicken stock*	*125 ml/3 fl oz salsa*

In a small bowl, mix together the garlic, 1 tablespoon basil, the black pepper and olive oil. Lightly crush the garlic with the back of a spoon to release the juices into the oil. Let the mixture stand while you prepare the tomatoes.

Skin the tomatoes by dropping them into a pan of boiling water for about 40 seconds. Let them cool slightly, then slip off the skins. Cut them in half and squeeze out the seeds. Core and coarsely chop the tomatoes.

Put the tomatoes, chicken stock and garlic-oil mixture into a medium saucepan. Bring to the boil, then reduce the heat to low, and simmer, uncovered, for 1 hour. Add the remaining basil, the balsamic vinegar and salt, then purée the soup in a blender. Taste and adjust the seasonings. Chill until serving time.

Top each bowl of soup with 1 to 2 tablespoons red pepper salsa.

CORN CHOWDER

Serves 4

A classic chowder never loses its appeal. Prepare in advance and freeze in convenient portion sizes for ease.

INGREDIENTS

300 g/10 oz tinned sweetcorn, drained

600 ml/1 pt vegetable stock

1 red onion, diced

1 green pepper, seeded and diced

600 ml/1 pt skimmed milk

2 tbsp cornflour

200 g/7 oz low-fat Cheddar or Edam cheese, grated

1 tbsp fresh snipped chives

Ground black pepper

Snipped chives, to garnish

Place the sweetcorn, stock, onion and pepper in a pan. Blend 4 tablespoons of milk with the cornflour to form a paste.

Bring the pan contents to the boil, reduce the heat and simmer for 20 minutes. Add the milk and cornflour paste and bring to the boil, stirring until thickened. Stir in the cheese and chives and season. Heat until the cheese has melted, garnish and serve.

RED PEPPER SALSA

Makes about 375 ml/12 fl oz

INGREDIENTS

4 red peppers

2 x 1-cm/½-in-thick slices of onion, peeled

3 garlic cloves, unpeeled

2 Serrano chillies, chopped and partly seeded

2 tbsp olive oil

1 tbsp chopped fresh basil

1 tsp grated lemon rind

2 tbsp red wine vinegar

¼ tsp salt

To roast the peppers, cut them into 4 or 5 pieces lengthwise. Place the peppers, onion slices and unpeeled garlic on a barbecue or under the grill. The garlic should soften slightly, but needs to be watched closely as it scorches easily and turns bitter. The onions should be turned once, and should be softened and slightly browned. The skin of the peppers should be blistered and blackened, but take care not to char them so completely that the flesh is burned.

Remove the peppers from the fire or the grill as they blacken. As you remove them, place them in a polythene bag, or a covered bowl or wrap in foil. Pull the skin off the peppers after 10 minutes. Because they have a tendency to get stringy lengthwise, cut them into several strips across their width.

Peel the garlic cloves. Cut each onion slice into quarters. Put the peppers, onions and garlic into a blender or food processor with the remaining ingredients. Process until the ingredients are well chopped but not so finely chopped that the salsa turns into a paste. Taste and adjust the seasoning.

Corn Chowder ▶

COURGETTE AND MINT SOUP

Serves 4

This delicate soup may be served both hot or cold. If serving hot, stir in the yoghurt once the soup has been blended, garnish and serve immediately with hot bread or croutons.

INGREDIENTS

850 ml/1½ pt vegetable stock

1 onion, chopped

1 garlic clove, crushed

3 courgettes, grated

1 large potato, scrubbed and chopped

1 tbsp chopped fresh mint

Ground black pepper

150 ml/¼ pt plain yoghurt

Mint sprigs and courgette strips, to garnish

Put half the vegetable stock in a large saucepan, add the onion and garlic and cook for 5 minutes over a gentle heat until the onion softens. Add the shredded courgettes, potato and the remaining stock. Stir in the mint and cook over a gentle heat for 20 minutes or until the potato is cooked.

Let the soup cool slightly. Transfer the soup to a blender or food processor and blend lightly for 10 seconds, until almost smooth. Turn the soup into a bowl, season and stir in the yoghurt. Cover and chill for 2 hours. Spoon the soup into individual serving bowls or a soup tureen, garnish and serve.

NACHOS

Serves 3–4

Nachos are easy to make, and with real cheese and lots of extras they're better than most commercial versions. The joy of homemade nachos is that you can prepare them to suit your own taste. This deluxe version calls for tomatoes, avocados, olives, spring onions and salsa.

INGREDIENTS

350 g/11 oz tortilla chips

375 g/12 oz Cheddar cheese, grated

2 or 3 jalapeño chillies, cut crosswise into thin slices

2 medium tomatoes, seeded and chopped

50 g/2 oz chopped spring onions

75 g/3 oz black olives, pitted and sliced

1 large ripe avocado, peeled, stoned and diced

150 ml/¼ pt tomato-based salsa

Preheat the oven to 200°C/400°F/Gas 6. Mound the tortilla chips on one or two ovenproof serving platters, layering with the cheese and jalapeños. Bake until the cheese is melted, 3 to 5 minutes. Remove from the oven and sprinkle with the tomatoes, spring onions, olives and avocados. Serve with the salsa as a dip.

SQUASH SOUP

Serves 4

A smooth, thick stock is poured over bits of browned potato in this rich, yet inexpensive, soup.

INGREDIENTS

25 g/1 oz butter

125 g/4 oz chopped onion

1 garlic clove, crushed

2 baking potatoes, cubed but not peeled

2–3 squashes, sliced

750 ml/1¼ pt vegetable stock

Pinch of cayenne pepper

Pinch of ground black pepper

1 tsp paprika

½ tsp dried thyme

½ tsp dried basil

200 ml/6 fl oz single cream

Salt to taste

In a frying pan over medium heat, melt the butter. Sauté the onion and garlic until soft, about 5 minutes. Add the potatoes and sauté for 8 to 10 minutes. (You may need to add another 25 g/1 oz butter at this point.) Remove a cupful of potatoes and keep warm. Add the squash to the frying pan and sauté for about 3 minutes.

In a saucepan, mix together the stock and seasonings, then add the sautéed vegetables. Bring to the boil, then reduce the heat and simmer for about 40 minutes. Purée the soup in batches in a blender or food processor.

Return the puréed soup to the saucepan and heat through. Add the cream and salt to taste and heat through but do not boil. Divide the reserved potatoes among serving bowls and ladle the soup over the potatoes.

PINZIMONIO

Serves 4

INGREDIENTS

1 red pepper, cut into strips

1 bulb fennel, cut into strips and tossed lightly with lemon juice

1 head chicory, divided into spears

2–3 young artichoke hearts

½ cucumber, sliced

½–1 head radicchio, cored and leaves separated

4 celery stalks, cut into large pieces

Handful of rocket leaves

Baby carrots, blanched

4 ripe tomatoes, cut into wedges

Small bowl of good, fruity olive oil: allow 1–2 tbsp per person

3–4 tbsp balsamic vinegar per person

3–4 tbsp flaked or coarse grain sea salt per person

1–2 tbsp coarsely ground black pepper per person

1 lemon, cut into wedges

Cut the vegetables. Blanch the artichoke hearts if they have grown a choke and toss in lemon juice. Arrange the vegetables on a platter or in a basket. Diners at the table may want to chop their vegetables into pieces, so be sure to provide sharp knives.

Place the bowl of olive oil in the centre of the table. For each person, place a small saucer of balsamic vinegar, and small bowls of salt, pepper and lemon wedges on a plate so that they can mix their own sauce for the vegetables.

TAMARILLO AND AVOCADO COCKTAIL

Serves 4

An excellent appetizer, with an interesting blend of sweet and savoury flavours. The egg-shaped tamarillo fruit, also known as "tree tomato", is native to South America. It has a tough, bitter skin that must be peeled, and reveals golden pink flesh that is purple-tinged around the seeds.

INGREDIENTS

2 large ripe avocados

3 tamarillos

Shredded lettuce

125 g/4 oz soft cheese with herbs and
garlic

6 tbsp Greek yoghurt or soured cream

1 tsp caster sugar

3 spring onions, chopped

Peel the tamarillos thinly, halve them lengthwise and slice across. Arrange a little shredded lettuce among four individual plates.

Mix the cheese with the yoghurt or soured cream in a bowl. Sprinkle the caster sugar over the tamarillos, mix in the chopped spring onions and leave to stand for 15 minutes.

Quarter and peel the avocados and slice them across. Arrange the avocado slices on the lettuce, top with the tamarillo mixture and spoon over the cheese and yoghurt dressing.

CHEESE-STUFFED PEPPERS

Serves 4

This is a simple but attractive idea. A slice from each of the red and green peppers makes a colourful appetizer.

INGREDIENTS

150 g/5 oz mixed shelled nuts (peanuts, cashews, almonds, etc.)

Salt

Cayenne pepper

200 g/7 oz low-fat cream cheese

1 garlic clove, crushed

Ground black pepper

1 medium red pepper

1 medium green pepper

Wholemeal toast, to serve

Heat a non-stick frying pan over a medium heat until evenly hot then add the nuts and cook until browned on all sides. Scatter some salt and cayenne pepper over some kitchen paper, add the hot nuts and toss in the seasonings. Chop the nuts roughly when cooled.

Beat the cream cheese until smooth, then add the garlic and nuts. Season to taste with extra salt, if necessary, and black pepper. Cut the tops from the bell peppers and remove the seeds and cores. Pack the filling into the peppers, pressing it down firmly with the back of a spoon.

Chill the peppers for 2 to 3 hours before slicing. Serve one slice of each coloured pepper to each person, with wholemeal toast.

MIXED VEGETABLE TAGINE

Serves 4

Raisins may also be added to this dish, if liked. Include them with the vegetables.
Serve the tagine over couscous or rice.

INGREDIENTS

200 g/7 oz chickpeas, soaked overnight,
then drained and chopped

3 tbsp olive oil

4 small carrots, sliced

2 onions, chopped

3 garlic cloves, chopped

2 courgettes, sliced

1 tsp ground coriander

1 tsp ground cumin

3 tomatoes, chopped

600 ml/1 pt vegetable stock

Salt and pepper

Juice of 1 lemon

2 tbsp chopped fresh parsley, to garnish

4 spring onions, white part only,
finely chopped, to garnish

Cook the chickpeas in plenty of boiling water until just tender; the time will mainly depend on the age and variety of the chickpeas.

Meanwhile, heat the oil in a pan, add the carrots and fry until browned. Remove and reserve. Add the onion and garlic to the pan and cook gently until soft and golden. Add the pepper and courgettes and cook until softened. Stir in the spices and cook until fragrant, then add the tomatoes, carrots, stock and seasoning. Bring to the boil.

Drain the chickpeas, add to the vegetable mixture, cover and simmer for about 30 minutes until all the vegetables are tender. Stir in the lemon juice then sprinkle over the parsley and spring onions.

BAKED TOMATOES

Makes 4 large or 8 small servings

Baked tomatoes are often regarded as a garnish rather than a dish in their own right. Use tomatoes that are firm, not overripe and time the cooking so you are ready to eat them as soon as they come out of the oven. Make your own crisp breadcrumbs by toasting good bread then grinding it coarsely, rather than using bland, commercial breadcrumbs.

INGREDIENTS

4 large tomatoes, firm but ripe	150 g/5 oz dried breadcrumbs
Salt	2 tbsp chopped fresh basil or 2 tsp dried
2 tbsp olive oil	2 tbsp finely chopped spring onion
3 garlic cloves, crushed	90 g/3 oz grated Parmesan cheese

Preheat the oven to 220°C/425°F/ Gas 7. Lightly grease a shallow baking tin. Core the tomatoes and cut them in half. Lightly salt the cut sides, and turn the tomatoes cut side down on kitchen paper to drain while you prepare the topping.

Heat the oil in a small frying pan. Add the garlic and sauté for 1 to 2 minutes, stirring and watching carefully so it doesn't scorch. If the oil is very hot, you may want to remove the pan from the burner. Add the breadcrumbs, return the pan to the heat and cook for 2 minutes, stirring constantly. Add the herbs and onion, continue cooking for about 30 seconds and remove the pan from the heat. Stir in the Parmesan cheese.

Place the tomatoes, cut side up, on the lightly oiled baking tin. Divide the topping among them. Bake until the tomatoes lose their firmness but are not mushy, 15 to 20 minutes. Serve immediately.

TORTILLA WHEELS WITH PINEAPPLE SALSA

Serves 8

Tortillas make excellent appetizers because they can be stuffed, sliced and baked.
These tortilla wheels may also be served plain as finger food.

INGREDIENTS

For the filling

150 g/5 oz cream cheese

1 green chilli, seeded and finely chopped

2 tbsp chopped fresh coriander

4 tomatoes, seeded and finely chopped

4 spring onions, finely chopped

1 pepper, red or yellow, seeded and
finely chopped

125 g/4 oz Cheddar cheese, grated

Salt and ground black pepper

8 flour tortillas

For the salsa

1 tbsp black mustard seeds

1 orange

4 thick slices pineapple, fresh or tinned

1 small red onion, finely chopped

1 small green chilli, seeded and
finely chopped

2 tomatoes, diced

Beat the cream cheese until smooth then add all the other ingredients for the filling. Mix well and season to taste with salt and pepper. Divide the mixture among the tortillas, spreading it evenly. Place each tortilla on top of another, making four stacks of two, then roll them up tightly. Cover in cling film and chill for at least 2 hours.

Prepare the salsa while the tortilla rolls are chilling. Heat a non-stick frying pan until evenly hot, then add the mustard seeds and cook for 1 to 2 minutes, until the seeds begin to pop. Allow to cool. Grate the rind from the orange, then peel it and chop the flesh. Mix the orange flesh and rind with the mustard seeds and the other ingredients, seasoning to taste with salt and pepper. Allow the salsa to stand until required.

Preheat the oven to 200°C/400°F/Gas 6. Unwrap the tortillas and trim away the ends, then cut each roll into eight slices. Place on baking sheets and bake for 15 to 20 minutes, until well browned. Serve with the salsa.

LIGHT LUNCHES
AND SUPPERS

SPINACH PANCAKES

Serves 4

These light pancakes are made from a low-fat dough, and cook very quickly.

INGREDIENTS

For the pancakes

90 g/3 oz plain flour

150 ml/¼ pt water

1 tsp sunflower oil

For the filling

2 tbsp vegetable stock

1 small courgette, sliced

225 g/4 oz spinach, shredded

1 small onion, chopped

225 g/8 oz button mushrooms, sliced

½ red pepper, seeded

1 celery stalk, sliced

1 garlic clove, crushed

Pinch of ground nutmeg

For the sauce

150 ml/¼ pt skimmed milk

1 tbsp cornflour

150 ml/¼ pt vegetable stock

Ground black pepper

1 tbsp chopped fresh thyme

90 g/3 oz grated vegetarian cheese

½ tsp paprika

Sift the flour into a mixing bowl and make a well in the centre. Heat the water and oil to boiling point and pour into the flour, mixing to form a dough. Turn onto a floured surface and knead for 3 to 4 minutes.

Cut the mixture into four equal portions and roll each into a 15-cm/6-in round. Heat a heavy, non-stick frying pan over a medium heat. Put one of the pancakes into the pan and place another on top. Cook for 3 to 4 minutes, turning once when the bottom pancake begins to brown. Repeat with the remaining mixture. Cover and reserve.

Heat the stock in a saucepan and cook the vegetables, garlic and nutmeg for 7 to 8 minutes, stirring. Drain the mixture well. Blend 2 tablespoons of the milk to a paste with the cornflour. Put in a saucepan with the remaining milk, vegetable stock, seasoning, thyme and half of the cheese. Bring the mixture to the boil, stirring until thickened.

Heat the oven to 190˚C/375°F/Gas 5. Spoon the vegetable mixture onto one half of each pancake and roll up. Put in a shallow ovenproof dish, seam side down. Pour the sauce over the top and sprinkle with the remaining cheese and paprika. Cook in the oven for 15 minutes until golden brown.

PASTA CAPONATA

Serves 4

*Caponata is an Italian tomato and vegetable dish which is perfect to serve hot as a pasta sauce.
In this recipe dried penne have been used but any pasta shapes or noodles would work equally well.*

INGREDIENTS

1 large aubergine

Salt

150 ml/¼ pt vegetable stock

1 onion, halved and sliced

2 garlic cloves, crushed

500 g/1 lb chopped plum tomatoes

2 tbsp cider vinegar

4 celery stalks, chopped

50 g/2 oz green beans, trimmed

50 g/2 oz pitted green olives, halved

1 tbsp chopped fresh basil

Ground black pepper

500 g/1 lb dried penne

Basil leaves, to garnish

Cut the aubergine into chunks and put in a colander. Sprinkle with salt and leave to stand for 20 minutes. Wash under cold water and pat dry. Cook the aubergine under a medium grill for 5 minutes, turning until browned.

Meanwhile, heat the stock in a saucepan and add the onion and garlic. Cook for 2 to 3 minutes until softened. Stir in the tomatoes, vinegar, celery and beans. Cook over a gentle heat for 20 minutes, stirring occasionally. Add the aubergine, olives and basil, season and cook for a further 10 minutes.

Meanwhile, cook the penne in boiling salted water for 8 to 10 minutes or until *al dente* (firm to the bite). Drain well and toss into the sauce. Spoon into a warmed serving dish, garnish with basil and serve.

CHESTNUT HASH

Serves 4

Cook the potatoes for this dish in advance or use up any leftover cooked potatoes for speed.

Allow the potato to brown on the base of the pan for a crunchier texture.

INGREDIENTS

1.5 kg/1½ lb potatoes, peeled and cubed	1 tsp paprika
1 red onion, halved and sliced	2 tbsp chopped fresh parsley
125 g/4 oz mange tout	300 ml/½ pt vegetable stock
125 g/4 oz broccoli florets	90 g/3 oz chestnuts, cooked, peeled and
1 courgette, sliced	quartered
1 green pepper, seeded and sliced	Ground black pepper
125 g/4 oz drained, tinned sweetcorn	Parsley sprigs, to garnish
2 garlic cloves, crushed	

Cook the potatoes in boiling water for 20 minutes or until softened. Drain well and reserve.

Meanwhile, cook the remaining ingredients in a frying pan for 10 minutes, stirring. Add the drained potatoes to the frying pan and cook for a further 15 minutes, stirring and pressing down with the back of a spoon. Serve immediately with bread.

VEGETABLE JAMBALAYA

Serves 4

This classic Caribbean dish is usually made with spicy sausage but this vegetarian version packs just as much of a punch and tastes wonderful.

INGREDIENTS

60 g/2 oz long-grain white rice

60 g/2 oz wild rice

1 aubergine, sliced and quartered

1 tsp salt

1 onion, chopped

1 celery stalk, trimmed and sliced

200 ml/7 fl oz vegetable stock

2 garlic cloves, crushed

200 g/7 oz baby corn

200 g/7 oz green beans, trimmed

200 g/7 oz baby carrots

225 g/8 oz tinned chopped tomatoes

4 tsp tomato purée

1 tsp creole seasoning

1 tsp chilli sauce

Chopped fresh parsley, to garnish

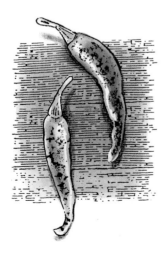

Cook the rices in boiling water for 20 minutes or until cooked. Drain well. Meanwhile, place the aubergine pieces in a colander, sprinkle with the salt and leave to stand for 20 minutes. Wash and pat dry with kitchen paper.

Put the aubergine, onion, celery and stock in a non-stick pan and cook for 5 minutes, stirring. Add the garlic, corn, beans, carrots, tomatoes, tomato purée, creole seasoning and chilli sauce. Bring the mixture to the boil, reduce the heat and cook for 20 minutes more until the vegetables are just cooked. Stir in the drained rice and cook for a further 5 minutes.. Garnish with parsley and serve.

GARLIC AUBERGINE CIABATTA ROLLS

Serves 8

These may take a little preparation but they are well worth the effort. Cooking garlic in its skin takes away the strong flavour and produces a milder garlic purée. This can be cooked in advance with the aubergine and gently warmed through to make the rolls.

INGREDIENTS

8 garlic cloves	2 tbsp basil leaves, shredded
1 aubergine, sliced	4 lettuce leaves, shredded
1 tbsp sunflower oil	4 ciabatta or large crusty rolls
125 g/4 oz sun-dried tomatoes	

Preheat the oven to 200°C/400°F/Gas 6. Put the garlic and aubergine slices on a non-stick baking sheet and cook in the oven for 30 minutes until soft. Remove from the oven and cool.

Squeeze the garlic purée from the cloves, mix in with the sunflower oil and reserve. Mix the reconstituted sliced tomatoes, basil and lettuce leaves together. Heat the rolls in a warm oven for 2 to 3 minutes and slice in half. Spread the garlic purée onto one half of each roll and top with the aubergine slices. Add the tomato mixture and top with remaining roll halves. Serve hot. Garnish with sliced tomatoes.

CHINESE NOODLES

Serves 4

This is a really quick and easy dish for a speedy lunch or supper. Use egg or rice noodles for a Chinese flavour or fresh
tagliatelle if preferred. If using dried pasta, it will need to cook for 8 to 10 minutes.

INGREDIENTS

225 g/8 oz thin egg or rice noodles	1 courgette, sliced
100 ml/3 fl oz vegetable stock	1 celery stalk, sliced
2 garlic cloves, crushed	1 tsp curry powder
1 red onion, halved and sliced	3 tbsp dark soy sauce
2.5-cm/1-in piece of ginger root, shredded	3 tbsp plum sauce
	1 tsp fennel seeds
1 red chilli, chopped	Chopped fresh parsley or fennel leaves,
2 carrots, cut into strips	to garnish
200 g/7 oz mange tout	

Cook the noodles in boiling water for 3 minutes. Drain and reserve. Meanwhile, heat the stock in a non-stick wok or frying pan and stir-fry the vegetables and spices for 3 to 4 minutes.

Add the drained noodles to the pan with the soy and plum sauces and the fennel seeds. Cook for 2 to 3 minutes, tossing well, and serve garnished with parsley or fennel leaves.

CYPRIOT SALAD

Serves 4

A Cypriot salad contains many greens – caper stems, lightly pickled wild seaweed, rocket; shredded white, green, or red cabbage, purslane, coriander. You never know what greens will appear in your evening salad, as the Cypriots are avid, daily hunters of wild herbs and salad leaves, and all of these go into their food. The only constant ingredients are the glistening, rich olive oil and lemon wedges for you to squeeze on as you like.

INGREDIENTS

½–1 small white cabbage, shredded	*Extra-virgin olive oil, as desired*
Handful of rocket leaves, chopped	*Juice of 1 lemon, plus extra lemon halves, to serve*
3–4 tbsp chopped fresh coriander	
1–2 tbsp chopped fresh parsley	*Salt and black pepper to taste*
Wild greens, as available (optional, see above)	*5–6 ripe, juicy tomatoes, quartered*
	10 or more black olives
1 cucumber, diced	*10 or more green olives*
1 bunch spring onions, thinly sliced	*125 g/4 oz feta cheese, cut into slices*
Mint leaves, thinly sliced (optional)	

Combine the cabbage, rocket, coriander, parsley, wild greens (if using), cucumber, spring onions and mint. Toss with olive oil, lemon, salt and pepper then arrange in a bowl.

Top with tomato wedges, black and green olives and feta, and serve with more olive oil and lemon.

TABBOULEH

Serves 6

A traditional tabbouleh is almost green in colour from the high proportion of herbs to bulgur wheat. It is important to dry the wheat thoroughly or the finished salad will be soggy and unpalatable.

INGREDIENTS

150 g/5 oz fine bulgur wheat
150 ml/¼ pt boiling water
2 tbsp chopped fresh parsley
2 tbsp chopped fresh mint
2 tomatoes, seeded and chopped
2 spring onions, trimmed and finely chopped
½ cucumber, diced
Juice of 1 lime
Salt and ground black pepper
60 ml/2 fl oz fruity olive oil

Allow the bulgur wheat to soak in the boiling water for 30 minutes then drain, if necessary, and squeeze dry in a clean tea towel.

Place the wheat in a large bowl and add all the remaining ingredients, including seasonings to taste. Toss the salad well and serve at room temperature.

Cypriot Salad ▶

AUBERGINE PATE

Serves 6

A creamy pâté to serve with toast, crusty bread, crackers or crudités.

INGREDIENTS

1 large or 2 small aubergines

250 g/8 oz cream cheese

1 garlic clove, crushed

1 green chilli, seeded and chopped

1 tbsp tomato purée

Salt and ground black pepper

Paprika, to sprinkle

Cook the aubergine over a barbecue, under a grill, or in a hot oven until the skin is wrinkled and blistered and the flesh is tender. Turn once or twice during cooking. Cover with a damp cloth and leave to cool for about 10 minutes, then peel off the skin.

Blend the aubergine with the remaining ingredients in a food processor. Season well, then turn into a serving bowl. Sprinkle with paprika. Chill for 30 minutes before serving.

SQUASH RISOTTO WITH BLUE CHEESE AND PECANS

Serves 4

A brilliant, unusual risotto. If you wish, use a piquant blue cheese such as Stilton to give a tangy, sharp zing. However, a sweeter cheese, such as dolcelatte, will give a more subtle flavouring. The pecans add an interesting crunch.

INGREDIENTS

Good pinch of saffron threads

1¼ l/2 pt well-flavoured vegetable stock

2 tbsp olive oil

Knob of butter

1 onion, finely chopped

500 g/1 lb peeled, seeded and diced squash, such as acorn or Hubbard

2 garlic cloves, crushed

375 g/12 oz arborio rice

12 sage leaves, shredded

250 g/8 oz crumbled blue cheese

250 g/8 oz pecans, chopped

Salt and ground black pepper

Dressed rocket leaves, to garnish

Soak the saffron in the almost boiling stock until required – keep the stock as warm as possible. Heat the oil and butter together in a large frying pan, then add the onion and cook over a low heat until softened but not browned.

Add the squash and cook quite quickly, until almost starting to brown, stirring all the time. Stir in the garlic and the rice and toss to coat in oil.

Add one third of the stock, then bring the rice to the boil and cook, stirring frequently, until almost all the stock has been absorbed. Add half the remaining stock and repeat the cooking process, then add the sage leaves followed by the remaining stock. Continue cooking until almost all the stock has been absorbed then stir in the crumbled blue cheese and the chopped pecans.

Continue cooking until the cheese has just melted, then remove the pan from the heat and season the mixture well, according to taste. Serve garnished with dressed rocket leaves.

AUBERGINE-STUFFED MUSHROOMS

Serves 4

The aubergine purée for this recipe can be made in advance and stored in the refrigerator for up to one day.

INGREDIENTS

1 aubergine	1 tbsp chopped fresh coriander
2 garlic cloves, crushed	8 large open cap mushrooms, peeled
Juice of 1 lime	50 g/2 oz vegetarian cheese, grated
250 g/8 oz wholemeal breadcrumbs	4 tbsp vegetable stock
1 tbsp tomato purée	Coriander to garnish

Preheat the oven to 220°C/425°F/Gas 7. Cut the aubergine in half lengthwise and place skin side uppermost in a baking dish. Cook in the oven for 30 minutes until soft. Remove the aubergine from the oven and leave to cool. Scoop the soft flesh from the skin and put in a food processor with the garlic and lime juice. Add the breadcrumbs to the food processor with the tomato purée and coriander and blend for 10 seconds to mix well.

Spoon the purée onto the mushrooms pressing the mixture down. Sprinkle the cheese on top and transfer the mushrooms to a shallow ovenproof dish. Pour the stock around the mushrooms, cover and cook in the oven for 20 minutes. Uncover and cook for a further 5 minutes until golden on top.

Remove the mushrooms from the oven and lift out of the dish with a slotted spoon. Serve with a mixed salad and garnish with coriander.

SQUASH-STUFFED ROAST PEPPERS

Serves 4

The combination of peppers and squash is a very happy culinary experience. Red peppers are much sweeter than green for baking or roasting; yellow are the next best.

INGREDIENTS

4 large red peppers	4 fresh tomatoes, skinned, halved and seeded
375 g/12 oz peeled, seeded, and diced, firm-fleshed squash, such as acorn	300 ml/½ pt single cream
2 large garlic cloves, finely sliced	125 g/4 oz grated Parmesan cheese
Salt and ground black pepper	Olive oil

Pre-heat the oven to 220°C/ 425°F/ Gas 7. Cut the peppers in half lengthwise—try to cut through the stalk and leave it in place as this will help to keep the peppers in shape. Remove the core and seeds, then rinse the peppers and arrange them in a suitable ovenproof dish or small roasting tin.

Pile the diced squash into the peppers, burying the sliced garlic in among the pieces. Season well then top with the halved tomatoes.

Mix the cream with the Parmesan cheese and a little more seasoning, then carefully pour the mixture into the peppers.

Drizzle a little olive oil over, then bake at the top of the hot oven for 30 to 35 minutes, until the peppers are starting to blacken and the cheese is browned.

Serve hot with fresh salad leaves or some stir-fried courgettes.

ROASTED VEGETABLES ON TOAST

Serves 4

The flavour of roasted vegetables is quite different from that achieved by boiling or steaming, and one not to be missed. This Mediterranean mixture is very colourful and enhanced by the light cheese sauce.

INGREDIENTS

1 bulb of fennel, trimmed and quartered	**For the sauce**
2 open cap mushrooms, peeled and sliced	150 ml/¼ pt vegetable stock
1 courgette, sliced	90 ml/3 fl oz skimmed milk
1 red pepper, halved, seeded and sliced	2 garlic cloves, crushed
1 red onion, cut into eight pieces	50 g/2 oz low-fat cream cheese
1 tbsp sunflower oil	Ground black pepper
2 rosemary sprigs	1 tsp Dijon mustard
8 small slices of thick wholemeal bread	1 tbsp cornflour
	1 rosemary sprig, chopped
	Basil leaves and rosemary sprigs, to garnish

Preheat the oven to 200°C/400°F/Gas 6. Blanch all the vegetables in boiling water for 8 minutes and drain well. Transfer the vegetables to a roasting tin and sprinkle the oil and rosemary over the top. Cook in the oven for 25 minutes or until softened and beginning to char slightly.

Meanwhile, heat the stock for the sauce in a pan with the milk. Add the garlic, cream cheese, ground black pepper and mustard. Blend the cornflour with 2 tablespoons of cold water to form a paste and stir into the sauce. Bring to the boil, stirring until thickened, and add the rosemary sprigs.

Toast the bread under the grill for 2 to 3 minutes each side until golden. Arrange two slices of the toast on four warmed serving plates and top with the roasted vegetables. Spoon over the sauce, garnish with basil and rosemary and serve immediately.

VEGETABLE ENCHILADAS

Serves 4

This is a vegetarian version of the Mexican dish.

INGREDIENTS

2 flour tortillas

For the filling

125 g/4 oz spinach, stems removed

4 spring onions, sliced

*50 g/2 oz grated vegetarian cheddar
cheese*

Pinch of ground coriander

1 small celery stalk, trimmed and sliced

90 g/3 oz drained, tinned sweetcorn

1 carrot, peeled and grated

For the sauce

150 ml/¹/₄ pt skimmed milk

2 tbsp cornflour

150 ml/¹/₄ pt vegetable stock

4 pickled Jalapeño chillies, sliced

125 g/4 oz grated vegetarian cheese

1 tbsp tomato purée

1 tbsp chopped basil

Basil leaves or coriander sprigs, to garnish

Blanch the spinach for the filling in boiling water for 2 to 3 minutes. Drain well and put in a mixing bowl with the spring onions, cheese, coriander, celery, sweetcorn and carrot.

Spoon half of the filling along one edge of each of the tortillas. Roll up the tortillas and cut in half. Put in a shallow ovenproof baking dish, seam side down.

To make the sauce, blend 4 tablespoons of the skimmed milk to a paste with the cornflour. Heat the remaining milk and vegetable stock in a saucepan and stir in the cornflour paste, jalapeño chillies, half of the cheese and the tomato purée. Bring the sauce to the boil, stirring until thickened. Cook for 1 minute and pour over the tortillas in the dish.

Sprinkle the remaining cheese on top and cook in the oven at 175˚C/350°F/ Gas 4 for 30 minutes or until the sauce is bubbling and the cheese has melted and is lightly golden. Garnish with basil or coriander and serve with a small fresh salad.

VEGETARIAN CLASSICS

VEGETABLE AND TOFU PIE

Serves 8

In this recipe, firm tofu (bean curd) is cubed and added to the pie. If liked, use a marinated tofu for extra flavour and use in the same way.

INGREDIENTS

4 sheets of filo pastry	250 g/8 oz cauliflower florets
1 tbsp polyunsaturated low-fat spread, melted	125 g/4 oz fine green beans, halved
	2 celery stalks, sliced
	250 g/8 oz firm tofu, diced
For the filling	300 ml/½ pt vegetable stock
1 leek, sliced	2 tbsp chopped fresh coriander
2 garlic cloves, crushed	Ground black pepper
2 carrots, diced	1 tbsp cornflour

Place all the vegetables and tofu in a non-stick frying pan and dry-fry for 3 to 5 minutes, stirring. Add the stock and coriander, season and cook for 20 minutes or until the vegetables are tender. Blend the cornflour to a smooth paste with 2 tablespoons of cold water, add to the mixture and bring the mixture to the boil, stirring until thickened.

Spoon the mixture into an ovenproof pie dish. Lay one sheet of filo pastry on top and brush with melted fat. Cut the remaining pastry into strips and lay on top, folding as you go to create a rippled effect. Sprinkle the remaining fat on top and bake the pie in the oven at 200°C/400°F/Gas 6 for 20 minutes until golden brown. Serve with new potatoes.

MIXED BEAN CHILLI

Serves 4

Chilli con carne has always been a warming favourite dish, and this recipe without the 'carne' is no exception.
Packed with vegetables and beans, it is a fully satisfying meal.

INGREDIENTS

500 g/1 lb tinned beans such as borlotti,
red kidney, black-eyed, and pinto beans,
drained

400-g/14-oz tin chopped tomatoes

1 tbsp tomato purée

1 onion, halved and sliced

150 g/5 oz cubed potatoes

1 green pepper, seeded and chopped

200 g/7 oz halved baby corn

2 green chillies, seeded and chopped

1 tsp chilli powder

2 garlic cloves, crushed

150 ml/¼ pt vegetable stock

Chopped fresh parsley, to garnish

Place all the ingredients except the garnish in a large saucepan and bring to the boil. Reduce the heat, cover the pan, and simmer for 45 minutes or until all the vegetables are cooked and the juices have thickened slightly. Stir the chilli occasionally while cooking.

Garnish with parsley and serve with brown rice or baked potatoes.

VEGETABLE FLAN

Serves 4

This flan, made with low-fat pastry filled with vegetables and low-fat cheese, is delicious served hot.

INGREDIENTS

For the pastry

125 g/4 oz flour

2 tbsp skimmed milk

1½ tsp baking powder

1 tsp mustard powder

For the filling

1 celery stalk, sliced

125 g/4 oz button mushrooms, sliced

2 baby corn cobs, sliced

1 leek, sliced

2 garlic cloves, crushed

8 asparagus spears, trimmed

125 ml/3 fl oz vegetable stock

125 g/4 oz cottage cheese

150 ml/¼ pt skimmed milk

1 egg white, beaten

Preheat the oven to 200°C/400°F/ Gas 6. Mix the pastry ingredients in a bowl and add enough cold water to bring the mixture together to form a soft dough. Roll the pastry out on a lightly floured surface to fit a 20-cm/8-in pie dish.

Cook the prepared vegetables in the stock for 5 minutes, stirring. Remove from the pan with a slotted spoon and place in a bowl. Add the cottage cheese, milk and egg white. Spoon the mixture into the pastry case and cook for 40 minutes until set and golden brown. Serve hot with a crisp salad.

STUFFED PASTA SHELLS

Serves 4

INGREDIENTS

16 large pasta shells	**For the filling**
	4 tbsp vegetable stock
For the sauce	1 courgette, diced
1 400-g/14-oz tin chopped tomatoes	50 g/2 oz tinned or frozen sweetcorn
2 garlic cloves, crushed	1 green pepper, seeded and diced
1 tbsp chopped fresh parsley	125 g/4 oz button mushrooms, sliced
1 onion, chopped	1 leek, sliced
2 tbsp tomato purée	2 garlic cloves, crushed
Ground black pepper	1 tbsp chopped fresh mixed herbs
	Basil leaves, to garnish

Place the sauce ingredients in a pan, bring to the boil, cover and simmer for 10 minutes. Transfer to a blender and blend for 10 seconds. Return the sauce to the pan and heat through. Meanwhile, put all the filling ingredients, except the herbs, in a saucepan and cook for 10 minutes, simmering until the vegetables are tender. Stir in the herbs and season.

Cook the pasta in boiling salted water for 8 to 10 minutes until just tender and drain well. Spoon the vegetable filling into the pasta shells and arrange on warmed serving plates. Spoon the sauce around the shells, garnish with basil and serve.

VEGETABLE CHOP SUEY

Serves 4

Add a Chinese touch to your table with this simple recipe.

INGREDIENTS

300 ml/½ pt vegetable stock	1 green pepper, seeded and cut into
1 tsp Chinese five-spice powder	chunks
3 carrots, cut into strips	50 g/2 oz open cap mushrooms, sliced
3 celery stalks, sliced	375 g/ 12 oz beansprouts
1 red onion, sliced	1 tbsp light soy sauce

Pour the vegetable stock into a large frying pan or wok with the Chinese five-spice powder and cook all the vegetables except the mushrooms and beansprouts for 5 minutes.

Add the mushrooms, beansprouts, and soy sauce to the pan and cook for a further 5 minutes, stirring well. Serve immediately with boiled brown rice.

WILD RICE AND LENTIL CASSEROLE

Serves 4

This dish is superb on a cold day as it is really hearty and warming. To check that the rice is cooked, look at the ends to be sure they have split open, otherwise cook for a little longer until it is visibly cooked through.

INGREDIENTS

250 g/8 oz red split lentils

90 g/3 oz wild rice

1 l/1¾ pt vegetable stock

1 red onion, cut into eight pieces

2 garlic cloves, crushed

1 400-g/14-oz tin chopped tomatoes

1 tsp ground coriander

1 tsp ground cumin

1 tsp chilli powder

Salt and ground black pepper

90 g/3 oz button mushrooms, sliced

1 green pepper, seeded and sliced

125 g/4 oz broccoli florets

75 g/3 oz halved baby corn

1 tbsp chopped fresh coriander

Coriander sprigs, to garnish

Cook the lentils and wild rice in the vegetable stock in a large flameproof casserole dish for 20 minutes, stirring occasionally.

Add the onion, garlic, tomatoes, spices, mushrooms, pepper, broccoli and corn. Bring the mixture to the boil, reduce the heat and cook for a further 15 minutes until the rice and lentils are thoroughly cooked. Add the chopped coriander, garnish and serve immediately with warm crusty bread.

WINTER VEGETABLE CASSEROLE

Serves 4

Use whatever vegetables you have to hand for this recipe as long as there is a good mixture. Cauliflower helps to thicken the sauce slightly so it is always best to include it.

INGREDIENTS

2 large potatoes, sliced

900 ml/1½ pt vegetable stock

2 carrots, cut into chunks

1 onion, sliced

2 garlic cloves, crushed

2 parsnips, sliced

1 leek, sliced

2 celery stalks, sliced

250 g/8 oz cauliflower florets

Salt and ground black pepper

1 tsp paprika

2 tbsp chopped mixed herbs

50 g/2 oz grated vegetarian cheese

Cook the potatoes in boiling water for 10 minutes. Drain well and reserve. Meanwhile, heat 300 ml/½ pt of the stock in a flameproof casserole dish. Add all the vegetables, remaining stock, seasoning and paprika, and cook for 15 minutes stirring occasionally. Add the herbs and adjust the seasoning.

Lay the potato slices on top of the vegetable mixture and sprinkle the cheese on top. Cook in the oven at 190°C/ 375°F/Gas 5 for 30 minutes or until the top is golden brown and the cheese has melted. Serve with a crisp salad.

ROASTED PEPPER TART

Serves 8

This is one of those dishes that are as appealing to the eye as to the palate. A medley of roasted peppers in a cheese sauce are served in a crisp filo pastry shell. For a dinner party, make individual pastry shells and serve the tarts with a small salad.

INGREDIENTS

250 g/8 oz filo pastry

250 g/8 oz margarine, melted

For the filling

2 red peppers, halved and seeded

2 green peppers, halved and seeded

2 garlic cloves, crushed

For the sauce

300 ml/½ pt milk

50 g/2 oz grated vegetarian cheese

2 tbsp cornflour

60 ml/2 fl oz vegetable stock

1 tbsp snipped fresh chives

1 tbsp chopped fresh basil

1 garlic clove, crushed

1 tsp wholegrain mustard

Basil leaves and snipped chives, to garnish

Lay two sheets of filo pastry in a pie plate allowing the pastry to overhang the sides a little. Brush with margarine and lay another two sheets on top at opposing angles. Brush with margarine and continue in this way until all of the pastry has been used. Heat the oven to 200°C/400°F/Gas 6 and cook the pastry shell for 15 minutes until golden and crisp.

Meanwhile, lay the peppers on a baking sheet, skin side uppermost. Sprinkle the garlic over the peppers and cook in the oven for 20 minutes. Leave to cool slightly then peel the peppers, discarding the skin. Cut the peppers into strips and place in the pastry shell.

Heat the milk for the sauce in a pan, add the cheese and stir until melted. Blend the cornflour with 4 tablespoons cold water to form a paste and stir, with the stock, into the sauce. Bring to the boil, stirring until thickened and add the remaining ingredients. Spoon the sauce over the peppers, garnish with basil and chives and serve.

PASTA TIMBALE

Serves 8

*This is a different way to serve pasta in a courgette-lined mould which is baked
until set and served with a tomato sauce.*

INGREDIENTS

2 courgettes	2 tbsp drained, tinned sweetcorn	**For the sauce**
250 g/8 oz pasta shapes such as macaroni or penne	1 green pepper, seeded and chopped	1 onion, chopped
60 ml/2 fl oz vegetable stock	50 g/2 oz grated vegetarian cheese	1 lb tomatoes, chopped
2 onions, chopped	1 400-g/14-oz tin chopped tomatoes	2 tsp granulated sugar
2 garlic cloves, crushed	2 eggs, beaten	2 tbsp tomato purée
1 carrot, chopped	2 tbsp chopped fresh oregano	225 ml/7 fl oz vegetable stock

Cut the courgettes into thin strips with a vegetable peeler and blanch in boiling water for 2 to 3 minutes. Refresh the courgettes under cold water, then put in a bowl and cover with cold water until required.

Cook the pasta in boiling salted water for 8 to 10 minutes until just tender. Drain well and reserve.

Heat the stock in a saucepan and cook the onions, garlic, carrot, sweetcorn and peppers for 5 minutes. Stir in the pasta, cheese, tomatoes, eggs and oregano, season well and cook for 3 minutes, stirring well.

Line a 1¼-l/2-pt mould or round tin with the courgette strips, covering the base and sides and allowing the strips to overhang the sides. Spoon the pasta mixture into the mould and fold the courgette strips over the pasta to cover.

Stand the mould in a roasting tin half filled with boiling water, cover and cook in the oven at 175°C/350°F/Gas 4 for 30 to 40 minutes until set.

Meanwhile, put all the sauce ingredients in a pan and bring to the boil,

then reduce the heat and cook for a further 10 minutes. Strain the sauce into a clean pan and heat gently.

Remove the pasta dish from the oven and carefully unmould onto a serving plate. Serve with the tomato sauce.

VEGETABLE GRATIN

Serves 4

INGREDIENTS

2 leeks, cut into strips lengthwise	¼ tsp freshly grated nutmeg
2 carrots, cut into sticks	150 ml/¼ pt apple juice
125 g/4 oz mange tout	150 ml/¼ pt vegetable stock
125 g/4 oz baby corn, halved	250 g/8 oz fresh white breadcrumbs
2 garlic cloves, crushed	2 tbsp chopped fresh coriander
1 tbsp clear honey	50 g/2 oz grated cheese
½ tsp ground ginger	

Place the vegetables in a large pan of boiling water and cook for 10 minutes. Drain well and place in a shallow ovenproof dish. Mix together the garlic, honey, ginger, nutmeg, apple juice and stock and pour over the vegetables.

Mix together the breadcrumbs and coriander. Sprinkle over the vegetables to cover. Top with the cheese. Bake at 200°C/400°F/Gas 6 for 45 minutes or until golden brown. Serve immediately.

TOFU BURGERS AND FRENCH FRIES

Serves 4

Although not fries in the strictest sense, these potato sticks are baked to crispness in the oven.

INGREDIENTS

For the burgers

125 g/4 oz chopped carrots

125 g/4 oz shredded cabbage

1 onion, chopped

300 g/10 oz firm tofu (bean curd), cubed

1 tsp ground coriander

4 burger buns, split

Sliced tomatoes, lettuce and onion

For the french fries

2 large potatoes

2 tbsp flour

1 tbsp sunflower oil

Boil the carrots in water for 10 to 12 minutes until soft. Drain thoroughly. Cook the cabbage in boiling water for 5 minutes and drain well. Put the carrots, cabbage, onion, tofu and coriander in a food processor and process for 10 seconds. Using floured hands form the mixture into four equal-sized burgers. Chill in the refrigerator for 1 hour or until firm to the touch.

Cut the potatoes into thick french fries and cook in boiling water for 10 minutes. Drain well and toss in the flour.

Put the potatoes in a polythene bag and sprinkle in the oil. Seal the top of the bag and shake the fries to coat. Turn the potatoes out onto a non-stick baking sheet. Cook in the oven at 200°C/400°F/ Gas 6 for 30 minutes or until golden brown.

Meanwhile, place the burgers under a hot grill for 7 to 8 minutes, turning with a spatula. Toast the burger buns for 2 minutes and place a burger on one half. Add the tomatoes, lettuce and onion, top with the second half and serve with the fries.

Vegetable Gratin ▶

VEGETABLE PILAF

Serves 4

A pilaf is a spicy, fluffy rice. This recipe is packed with crisp vegetables, chestnuts and raisins and lightly coloured with saffron for a golden appearance. If you do not have saffron to hand, use a pinch of turmeric instead.

INGREDIENTS

2 tbsp sunflower oil

1 red onion, chopped

375 g/12 oz basmati rice

Few strands of saffron

50 g/2 oz sweetcorn

1 red pepper, seeded and diced

1 tsp curry powder

1 tsp chilli powder

1 green chilli, seeded and chopped

125 g/4 oz broccoli florets

600 ml/1 pt vegetable stock

125 g/4 oz cooked and peeled chestnuts, halved

90 g/3 oz raisins

For the sauce

150 ml/¼ pt plain yoghurt

2 tbsp chopped fresh mint

Pinch of cayenne pepper

Heat the oil in a frying pan and add the onion and rice. Cook for about 3 to 4 minutes, stirring. Add the remaining ingredients and bring the mixture to the boil. Reduce the heat and cook for 30 minutes more, stirring occasionally until the rice is cooked and the liquid absorbed.

Mix together the sauce ingredients and serve with the pilaf and a side salad.

POTATO AND CHEESE LAYER

Serves 4

This recipe uses half cream instead of single or double cream. If preferred, substitute with skimmed milk or vegetable stock.

INGREDIENTS

500 g/1 lb potatoes, thinly sliced

2 garlic cloves, crushed

50 g/2 oz grated cheese

1 onion, halved and sliced

2 tbsp chopped fresh parsley

60 ml/2 fl oz half cream

60 ml/2 fl oz skimmed milk

Ground black pepper

Chopped fresh parsley, to garnish

Cook the potatoes in boiling water for 10 minutes. Drain well. Arrange a layer of potatoes in the base of a shallow ovenproof dish. Add a little garlic, cheese, onion and parsley. Repeat the layers until all the potatoes, onion, cheese, garlic and parsley are used, finishing with a layer of cheese.

Mix together the half cream and milk. Season and pour over the potato layers. Bake at 160°C/325°F/Gas 4 for 1¼ hours until cooked through and golden brown. Sprinkle with black pepper, garnish with parsley and serve.

SAFFRON, PEPPER AND MARSALA RISOTTO

Serves 4

This colourful and fragrant risotto has the added sweetness of peppers and Marsala.

INGREDIENTS

2 medium red peppers	2 tbsp olive oil
2 medium yellow peppers	1 medium onion, finely chopped
2 medium green peppers	400 g/14 oz arborio (risotto) rice
4 tbsp Marsala	Large pinch of saffron
900 ml/1½ pt vegetable stock	Salt and ground black pepper

Preheat the grill. Halve and seed the peppers and grill for 7 to 8 minutes, turning occasionally, until the peppers are charred and softened. Carefully peel off the charred skin then slice into thin strips. Place in a shallow bowl and mix in the Marsala. Set aside.

Pour the stock into a saucepan and bring to the boil. Reduce the heat to a gentle simmer. Meanwhile, heat the oil in a large saucepan and gently fry the onion for 2 to 3 minutes until just softened, but not browned. Add the rice and cook, stirring, for 2 minutes until well coated in the onion mixture. Add a ladleful of stock and cook gently, stirring, until absorbed. Continue ladling the stock into the rice until half the stock is used and the rice becomes creamy. Sprinkle in the saffron and seasoning.

Continue adding the stock until the risotto becomes thick and the rice is tender. This will take about 25 minutes and should not be hurried. Stir in the pepper mixture and adjust the seasoning before serving.

VEGETABLE LASAGNE

Serves 4

INGREDIENTS

1 small aubergine

Salt

1 400-g/14-oz can chopped tomatoes

2 garlic cloves, crushed

1 tbsp chopped fresh basil

1 large courgette, chopped

1 onion, chopped

1 green pepper, seeded and chopped

125 g/4 oz button mushrooms, sliced

1 tsp chilli powder

Ground black pepper

125 g/4 oz green lasagne

(pre-cooked variety)

For the sauce

150 ml/¼ pt vegetable stock

300 ml/½ pt skimmed milk

50 g/2 oz grated vegetarian cheese

1 tsp Dijon mustard

2 tbsp cornflour

1 tbsp chopped fresh basil

Slice the aubergine and put in a colander. Sprinkle with salt and leave for 30 minutes. Wash and pat dry. Put the tomatoes, garlic, basil, courgette, onion, pepper, mushrooms and chilli powder in a saucepan. Add the aubergine, season and cook for 30 minutes, stirring occasionally until the vegetables are cooked.

Mix the stock for the sauce, the milk, half the cheese and the mustard in a saucepan. Blend the cornflour with 4 tablespoons cold water to form a paste and add to the pan. Bring to the boil, stirring until thickened.

Spoon a layer of the vegetable mixture into the base of an ovenproof dish. Lay half the lasagne on top to cover. Spoon on remaining vegetable mixture and cover with the remaining lasagne. Pour the cheese sauce over the top and bake at 190°C/375°F/Gas 5 for 40 minutes or until golden and bubbling. Sprinkle the basil on top and serve.

RATATOUILLE

Serves 4

A medley of vegetables cooked in a tomato and herb sauce. This is a strongly flavoured dish to be served with a plainer recipe or used to top baked potatoes.

INGREDIENTS

1 onion, halved and sliced

2 garlic cloves, crushed

150 ml/¼ pt vegetable stock

1 large aubergine, sliced

175 g/6 oz courgettes, sliced

1 yellow pepper, seeded and sliced

2 tbsp tomato purée

1 400-g/14-oz tin chopped tomatoes

175 g/6 oz tinned artichoke hearts, drained

2 tbsp chopped fresh oregano

Ground black pepper

Place the onion, garlic and stock in a frying pan and cook for 5 minutes until the onion softens. Add the aubergine, courgettes and yellow pepper and cook for a further 5 minutes.

Stir in the tomato purée, chopped tomatoes, artichoke hearts and 1 tablespoon of the oregano. Season well. Bring to the boil, cover and reduce the heat. Cook for 1 hour, stirring occasionally. Sprinkle with the remaining oregano and black pepper and serve.

LENTIL MOUSSAKA

Serves 4–6

A meatless variation of the classic baked dish. This is rich, filling and full of fibre, so it must be good for you!

INGREDIENTS

Olive oil, for frying

1 large onion, chopped

2 garlic cloves, crushed

1 green pepper, cored and chopped

250 g/8 oz red lentils

150 ml/¼ pt red wine

1 400-g/14-oz tin chopped tomatoes

Salt and ground black pepper

1 tbsp chopped fresh oregano

2 large aubergines, sliced

600 ml/1 pt milk

50 g/2 oz butter, plus extra for greasing

4 tbsp plain flour

250 g/8 oz grated Cheddar cheese

Preheat the oven to 220°C/425°F/Gas 7. In a large pan heat 2 tablespoons of oil. Add the onion, garlic and pepper and cook gently until soft. Add the lentils, red wine and tomatoes. Bring to the boil, then season and add the oregano. Simmer for 20 minutes, or until the lentils are soft. Add a little more wine to the sauce if it seems dry.

Meanwhile, heat 2 to 3 tablespoons of oil in a frying pan. Fry the aubergine slices on both sides until tender, adding more oil if necessary, then drain on kitchen paper. Add any oil left in the frying pan to the lentil sauce.

Heat the milk, butter and flour in a pan, stirring all the time, until boiling and thickened. Continue to cook for 1 minute, to remove the taste of flour from the sauce, then remove the pan from the heat. Add all but 2 tablespoons of the grated cheese and then season to taste.

Layer the lentil sauce and aubergine slices in a buttered, ovenproof dish, finishing with a layer of aubergine. Spoon the sauce over the aubergines, then scatter the remaining cheese over the top. Bake for 30 minutes, until the moussaka is browned and set. Serve with a salad and garlic bread.

SPICED CHICKPEAS

Serves 4

Chickpeas are a great source of carbohydrate and are important in a vegetarian diet.
Here they are simmered in a spicy tomato sauce and are delicious served with brown rice.

INGREDIENTS

200 g/7 oz chickpeas

1 tsp bicarbonate of soda

1 onion, halved and sliced

1 2.5-cm/1-in piece of ginger root, grated

4 tomatoes, chopped

1 green chilli, chopped

1 tsp curry powder

¹/₂ tsp chilli powder

1 tsp ground coriander

300 ml/¹/₂ pt vegetable stock

Chopped fresh coriander, to garnish

Put the chickpeas in a large mixing bowl with the bicarbonate of soda and enough water to cover. Leave to soak overnight. Drain the chickpeas and cover with fresh water in a large saucepan. Bring to the boil and boil rapidly for 10 minutes. Reduce the heat and simmer for 1 hour or until cooked.

Drain the chickpeas and put in a non-stick frying pan with the remaining ingredients. Cover and simmer for 20 minutes, stirring occasionally. Garnish with coriander and serve with brown rice.

MUSHROOM PASTA PIE

Serves 4

INGREDIENTS

500 g/1 lb puff pastry, thawed if frozen	*Dash of olive oil*	*40 g/1½ oz plain flour*
Milk, to glaze	*25 g/1 oz butter*	*150 ml/¼ pt milk*
	1 garlic clove, crushed	*Salt and ground black pepper*
For the filling	*125 g/4 oz button mushrooms, sliced*	*90 g/3 oz mature Cheddar cheese, grated*
250 g/8 oz dried wholemeal pasta shells	*About 12 baby corn, cut into chunks*	*Freshly chopped parsley, to garnish*

Preheat the oven to 200°C/400°F/Gas 6. Roll the pastry out into two rectangular pieces, each measuring 15 x 10 cm/6 x 4 in. Set one rectangle aside to make the base of the pastry shell. Take the other piece and cut out an inner rectangle using a ruler and a sharp knife, leaving a 2.5-cm/1-in border to make the rim of the pastry shell. Reserve the inner rectangle to make the lid and, using a sharp knife, score it to make a pattern. Brush a little milk around the edges of the base of the pastry shell, and place the rim in position on top.

Place on a baking sheet with the lid alongside, and brush all the surfaces with milk to glaze. Bake for about 15 to 20 minutes, or until well risen and golden brown. Remove from the oven, and transfer the pastry shell to a wire rack to cool. If the centre of the pastry shell has risen too high, gently press down to create a hollow space. Place on a serving plate.

To make the filling, bring a large saucepan of water to the boil and add the pasta shells with a dash of olive oil. Cook for 10 minutes, stirring occasionally, until tender. Drain well and set aside.

Melt the butter in a large saucepan, and sauté the garlic, mushrooms and baby corn for 5 to 8 minutes, or until softened. Stir in the flour. Gradually stir in the milk, stirring well after each addition. Bring the sauce slowly to the boil, stirring constantly to prevent lumps from forming. Season with salt and ground black pepper. Stir in the grated cheese and continue to cook for a further 2 to 3 minutes, until the cheese has melted.

Stir the pasta into the sauce, then spoon the sauce into the pastry shell. Sprinkle with the chopped fresh parsley, then place the lid on top and serve.

Pizza and Pasta

BASIC PIZZA DOUGH

Makes two 30-cm/12-in thin-crust pizzas or one deep-pan pizza

Basic pizza dough goes well with just about any topping you like. This is the classic Italian base.

INGREDIENTS

1 sachet active dry yeast	2 tbsp olive oil
300 ml/½ pt warm water	½ tsp salt
600 g/1¼ lb strong white flour	

1. Combine the yeast, warm water and 500 g/1 lb of the flour. Mix well to blend. Add the oil, salt and remaining flour and work until the dough sticks together.

2. Place the dough on a lightly floured surface. Dust your hands with flour and knead the dough until it is smooth and elastic, about 5 minutes. If the dough gets sticky, sprinkle it with a little flour.

3. Roll the dough into a ball and place it in a lightly oiled bowl. Cover the bowl with a clean tea towel and set in a warm, but not hot place to rise until doubled in volume, about 1 hour.

4. When the dough has risen, roll it into a ball to make one deep-pan pizza or divide it in two balls to make two 30-cm/12-in thin-crust pizzas. Before rolling out and topping the pizza, allow the dough to rest for 20 minutes.

5. When ready to bake, roll outwards toward the edges with the palm of your hand until the dough fills the pan evenly.

PIZZA SAUCE

Makes about 600 ml/1 pt sauce

Puréed tomatoes have the perfect consistency for pizza sauce. If you make extra sauce and freeze it, you'll always have some to hand.

INGREDIENTS

1 700-g/1¾-lb tin passata	1 tsp dried basil
1 bay leaf	1 tsp dried thyme
1 tsp dried oregano	½ tsp dried marjoram

Place all the ingredients in a pan and bring to the boil. Reduce the heat, cover loosely to keep from spattering and simmer for 30 minutes, stirring occasionally.

DEEP-PAN CREOLE PIZZA

Makes one 22 x 32-cm/9 x 13-in deep-pan pizza

Creole dishes tend to be spicy tomato and vegetable mixtures, and this pizza is no exception.
Okra is available from many supermarkets. It exudes a sticky liquid when cut,
which gives a viscous texture to the topping.

INGREDIENTS

1 quantity Basic Pizza Dough (see page 84)

250 g/8 oz okra

1 400-g/14-oz can chopped tomatoes

1 tsp dried oregano

1 tsp dried thyme

½ tsp dried basil

½ tsp cayenne pepper

2 garlic cloves, crushed

2 celery stalks, finely chopped

1 small onion, finely chopped

Preheat the oven to 260°C/500°F/Gas 10. Place the dough in the centre of a lightly oiled 32 x 22 x 5-cm/13 x 9 x 2-in pie tin. Using your fingers, gently spread the dough until it covers the base of the tin evenly and goes halfway up the sides.

Boil the okra until tender then chop. Put the tomatoes into a colander, drain and discard the liquid but reserve the thick sauce. Place the tomatoes and sauce in a bowl. Add the herbs, cayenne pepper and garlic. Add the celery and onions to the bowl. Finally, add the okra and stir gently to mix.

To assemble, spread the tomato and okra mixture onto the pizza dough and bake for 20 minutes.

PIZZA WITH CARAMELIZED ONIONS

Makes one 30-cm/12-in deep-pan pizza

Caramelized onions are cooked slowly in oil until they are golden brown and very soft. They have a wonderful flavour that works well on a pizza. Make them ahead of time and store them in the refrigerator until ready to use.

INGREDIENTS

1 quantity Basic Pizza Dough (see page 84)	*2 tsp red wine vinegar*
2 large onions	*175 ml/6 fl oz Pizza Sauce (see page 84)*
3 tbsp olive oil	*175 g/6 oz fontina cheese, grated*
½ tsp salt	

Preheat the oven to 260°C/500°F/Gas 10. Slice both ends off the onions but do not peel. Cut the onions in quarters. Place them skin side down in a roasting tin. Liberally brush each onion with 1 tablespoon of the oil and sprinkle with salt. Cover the tin with foil and bake for 30 minutes. After 30 minutes, remove the foil and brush the onion with the remaining oil. Sprinkle with vinegar. Turn the onion quarters on one side and return to the oven for 1 hour. Occasionally turn the onions and baste with the oil from the tin. When cooked, leave to cool or store in the refrigerator for later use.

When you are ready to assemble the pizza, slice the onion quarters into strips. Spread the pizza sauce over the pizza dough. Spread sliced onion over the sauce and top with cheese. Bake for 10 minutes.

PIZZA WITH ROASTED PEPPERS

Makes one 30-cm/12-in deep-pan pizza

Roasting peppers enhances their flavour, and once you've tried them on pizza, they'll become a favourite.

INGREDIENTS

1 quantity Basic Pizza Dough (see page 84)

1 red pepper

1 green pepper

1 yellow pepper

175 g/6 fl oz Pizza Sauce (see page 84)

90 g/3 oz fontina cheese, shredded

Preheat the oven to 260°C/500°F/Gas 10. Cut the tops off the peppers and remove the seeds. Cut the peppers in half and then squash them so that they lie relatively flat (don't worry if the edges tear). Place the peppers, skin side up, in a grill pan and grill for about 8 minutes until blackened. Using tongs, place the peppers in a polythene bag. Seal and leave to cool. Once cooled, the skin will peel off easily. Discard the skins and slice the roasted peppers into long strips.

Spread the pizza sauce over the pizza dough. Top with the pepper strips, alternating the colours. If any pepper strips are left over, cover them in olive oil, store in the refrigerator and they'll keep for several days (use them on other pizzas or in salads). Lightly cover the peppers with the cheese. The cheese should not be so thick that the colourful peppers are obscured. Bake for 10 minutes.

PIZZA PAELLA

Makes one 30-cm/12-in deep-pan pizza

In this vegetarian version of classic Spanish paella, leeks replace the fish and meat
but the traditional flavouring of saffron, garlic and onions is retained.

INGREDIENTS

1 quantity Basic Pizza Dough (see page 84)	Large pinch of saffron
1½ onions, roughly chopped	½ tsp salt
2 leeks	½ tsp cayenne pepper
2 tbsp olive oil	250 g/8 oz frozen peas, thawed
2 large garlic cloves, crushed	2–3 Italian plum tomatoes, chopped
1 tbsp lemon rind, cut in strips	50 g/2 oz black olives pitted and sliced

Preheat the oven to 260°C/500°F/Gas 10. Chop the leeks into 2.5-cm/1-in pieces. Heat the oil in a pan over a medium heat and add the onions, leeks, garlic, lemon rind, saffron, salt and cayenne pepper. Sauté for 5 minutes.

Remove from the heat and stir in the peas and tomatoes. Spread the mixture over the pizza dough. Top with the olives. Bake for 10 minutes.

INDIVIDUAL PESTO PIZZAS

Makes four 15-cm/6-in pizzas

Homemade pesto is so good it's worth growing a crop of basil in your garden in order to have a plentiful supply.
These pizzas make great appetizers, but also make a good main course for lunch.

INGREDIENTS

4 pieces of pitta bread	For the pesto sauce
1 small red onion, thinly sliced	Handful of fresh basil leaves, no stems
1 small tomato, thinly sliced	1 tbsp pine nuts
125 g/4 oz feta cheese, crumbled	1 large garlic clove, crushed
	60 ml/2 fl oz extra-virgin olive oil
	50 g/2 oz Parmesan cheese

First make the pesto sauce. Put the basil, pine nuts, garlic, olive oil and Parmesan cheese in a blender or food processor and mix until thoroughly blended. Make ahead of time and refrigerate if you wish.

To make the pizza, toast the pitta bread. Then top each piece with 1 tablespoon of pesto sauce, a slice of onion, a slice of tomato, and finally, an ounce of feta cheese.

Pizza Paella ▶

MINI COCKTAIL PIZZAS

Makes 8 mini pizzas

Use toasted muffins or a ready-baked base cut into small circles, as the recipe suggests.
These simple pizzas are pretty to look at as well as tasty to eat.

INGREDIENTS

1 ready-baked pizza base,
cut into 8 small circles

125 ml/4 fl oz Pizza Sauce (see page 84)

125 g/4 oz Gruyère cheese, grated

1 medium ripe tomato

2 tsp olive oil

4 tsp chopped fresh parsley

Spread pizza sauce on each pizza circle. Top with the cheese. Grill for 5 minutes, or until the cheese is bubbly and begins to turn golden brown.

Slice the tomato into thin rounds. Top each grilled pizza circle with one tomato slice. Brush with a little olive oil and sprinkle with about ½ teaspoon of parsley. Serve immediately.

SPINACH AND WALNUT MINI PIZZAS

Makes 12 mini pizzas

Walnut oil makes an unusual vinaigrette for this pizza. Choose a good-quality
Gorgonzola for the tangy, creamy topping.

INGREDIENTS

125 ml/4 fl oz walnut oil

225 g/8 oz walnut halves, broken

2 tbsp red wine vinegar

½ tsp salt

2 spring onions, finely chopped

6 baps or 1-2 ready-baked pizza bases,
cut into 12 small circles

125 g/4 oz fresh spinach, stems removed

175 g/6 oz Gorgonzola cheese

Pour the oil over the walnuts and marinate for about 15 minutes. Strain the walnuts and set aside. Mix the vinegar, salt and spring onions into the oil.

Lightly toast the baps. Wash the spinach and remove the stems. Pat dry and place a few leaves on each pizza circle. Top with a scant tablespoon of the dressing, 1 tablespoon of walnuts, and top with the cheese. Place under the grill for about 3 minutes until the cheese begins to melt.

◀ *Mini Cocktail Pizzas*

TOMATO AND MUSHROOM PIZZA

Serves 4

Tomatoes and mushrooms have a natural affinity. This pizza topping creates a wonderfully deep and rich flavour, which is lifted by the inclusion of fresh oregano.

INGREDIENTS

1 quantity Basic Pizza Dough (see page 84)

4 tbsp tomato purée (optional)

125 g/4 oz passata

2–3 fresh ripe or tinned

tomatoes, diced

1 garlic clove, crushed

1 tsp fresh oregano, crumbled

250 g/8 oz mushrooms, thinly sliced

375 g/12 oz mozzarella cheese, or half

mozzarella, half fontina, grated

2 tbsp olive oil

Freshly grated Parmesan

cheese, to taste

Preheat the oven to 200°C/400°F/Gas 6. Roll out the dough and use to line an oiled pizza dish. Spread the dough with the tomato purée, if using, then drizzle with the passata. Scatter the tomatoes, garlic, oregano, mushrooms and mozzarella cheese, or mozzarella and fontina cheeses, over the top. Drizzle with olive oil and sprinkle over Parmesan cheese.

Bake for 15 to 20 minutes, or until the cheeses have melted and the crust is golden.

CHEESE AND ARTICHOKE PIZZA

Makes one 30-cm/12-in double-crust pizza

Artichoke hearts bottled in olive oil are already marinated. Assemble the ingredients and bake them to produce a quick and perfectly seasoned pizza.

INGREDIENTS

1 quantity Basic Pizza Dough (see page 84)

1 300-g/10-oz bottle artichoke hearts

150 g/5 oz mozzarella cheese

150 g/5 oz grated fresh pecorino cheese

2 garlic cloves, crushed

50 g/2 oz tinned pimentos, drained

Preheat the oven to 260°C/500°F/Gas 10. Drain the artichoke hearts, reserving the liquid. Finely chop the artichoke and place in a bowl. Add both cheeses, garlic and drained pimentos. Measure 60 ml/ 2 fl oz of the reserved liquid from the

artichoke hearts and add it to the bowl. Stir to mix.

Top the pizza dough with the artichoke and cheese mixture and bake for 10 minutes, until the cheese is melted and golden.

Tomato and Mushroom Pizza ▶

PENNE AI FUNGHI

Serves 4

Sautéed mushrooms and asparagus pieces, simmered in a tomato-cream sauce, then tossed with quill-shaped penne and fresh basil, make an impressive pasta dish.

INGREDIENTS

1 onion, roughly chopped

4 garlic cloves, roughly chopped

3 tbsp olive oil or butter, plus a little extra to top

375 g/12 oz mixed mushrooms, cut into bite-sized pieces

Salt and ground black pepper

500 g/1 lb fresh tomatoes, finely chopped, or 250 g/8 oz tinned chopped tomatoes in their juice

¼–½ tsp sugar

375 ml/12 fl oz double cream

1–2 oz basil leaves, torn

12–16 oz penne

1 bunch thin asparagus, tough ends broken off, cut into bite-sized lengths

4–6 tbsp grated Parmesan cheese

Sauté the onion and garlic in the olive oil or butter, until softened and almost transparent. Add the mushrooms and cook, stirring occasionally to prevent sticking. Season with salt and pepper, then pour in the tomatoes and add the sugar. Bring to the boil and cook, stirring, for a few more minutes. Add the cream and about a third of the fresh basil. Taste, adjust the seasoning if necessary and remove from the heat.

Cook the pasta in a large pan of boiling salted water until half done, then add the asparagus and finish cooking. The pasta should be *al dente* (firm to the bite) and the vegetables just tender. Drain well.

Toss the hot pasta and asparagus with the creamy tomato-mushroom sauce, then toss with the Parmesan cheese, remaining basil and a little extra olive oil or butter. Serve piping hot on warmed plates with fresh crusty bread.

TOMATO SPAGHETTI WITH MUSHROOMS

Serves 4–6

For this dish you need to include at least one kind of dried mushroom as this will give the depth of flavour that is typical of Italian mushroom-based dishes. Dried porcini (ceps) keep well, and are an ingredient that no well-stocked kitchen should be without.

INGREDIENTS

For the sauce

1½ tbsp dried porcini mushrooms (ceps)

3 tbsp olive oil

1 red onion, peeled and cut into wedges

3–6 garlic cloves, thinly sliced

125 g/4 oz mushrooms, such as oyster or chanterelle, wiped and sliced

125 g/4 oz button mushrooms, wiped and sliced

6 tbsp red wine

2 tbsp extra-virgin olive oil

Salt and ground black pepper

2 tbsp chopped fresh sage

To serve

1 lb fresh tomato spaghetti

Chopped fresh sage

Soak the porcini in warm water for about 20 minutes. Drain, reserving the soaking liquid, and chop the porcini. Heat the oil in a pan and sauté the onion and garlic for 3 minutes. Add the chopped porcini, oyster (or chanterelle) and button mushrooms. Sauté for a further 5 minutes, stirring frequently.

Strain the porcini soaking liquid into the pan and add the red wine. Bring to the boil then simmer for 5 minutes or until the mushrooms are just cooked and the liquid has been reduced by about half. Stir in the extra-virgin oil, season to taste and add the sage. Cover, remove from the heat and reserve.

Meanwhile, cook the tomato spaghetti in plenty of boiling salted water for 3 to 4 minutes or until *al dente*. Drain and return to the pan. Add the mushrooms and sauce, and toss the ingredients lightly. Serve, garnished with the chopped fresh sage.

PASTA WITH SUN-DRIED TOMATO SALSA

Serves 4

The intense flavours of this powerful salsa may clash in concentrated form. When it is tossed with pasta, however, the flavours blend and become complementary.

INGREDIENTS

3 tbsp olive oil	1 tbsp chopped fresh basil
6 garlic cloves, crushed	4 bacon rashers, cooked and crumbled
1 tsp dried chillies	50 g/2 oz black olives, pitted and sliced
1 red pepper, cored, seeded and cut into quarters	375–500 g/12 oz–1 lb pasta
125 g/4 oz sun-dried tomatoes,	Grated Parmesan cheese

Heat the oil in a small frying pan over a low heat. Add the garlic and the dried chillies. Cook slowly, stirring often and pressing the garlic to release the juices, until the garlic is lightly browned, 5 to 8 minutes. The heat must be very low or the garlic may scorch and turn bitter. Remove from the heat and leave to stand while you prepare the other ingredients.

Cook the red pepper skin side down over a barbecue fire or skin side up under a grill until the skin is blackened. Remove from the heat and place it in a polythene bag to steam for 10 minutes. Peel off the skin and chop the flesh.

Chop the sun-dried tomatoes and put them into a small bowl with the basil. Add the bacon, garlic, chilli and olive oil mixture, red pepper and sliced olives. Cook the pasta in plenty of boiling salted water until just tender or *al dente*. Drain well, and then toss with the salsa and Parmesan cheese.

PASTA WITH COURGETTES, RICOTTA AND WALNUTS

Serves 4

A classic dish from the Liguria region of Italy, the richness of the nuts and the bland, milky, ricotta cheese are enhanced by the smooth fragrance of the olive oil.

INGREDIENTS

1 lb pappardelle

4–6 courgettes, sliced

4–6 garlic cloves, chopped

4 tbsp extra-virgin olive oil

250 g/8 oz ricotta cheese, crumbled

250 g/8 oz grated sharp cheese

90 g/3 oz walnuts, chopped into pieces

1–2 tsp fresh thyme leaves

Cook the pasta in rapidly boiling water for five minutes, then add the courgettes and continue cooking until *al dente*. Drain.

Toss the hot pasta and courgettes with the garlic, olive oil, ricotta and grated cheese, walnuts and thyme. Serve immediately.

WARM PASTA SALAD

Serves 4

*This salad combines the saltiness of green olives, the crunch of walnuts and the goodness of fresh vegetables.
Use freshly grated rather than packet Parmesan cheese – you'll notice a big difference in flavour. The flavours
are enhanced when this salad is served warm, but if you have any cold leftovers, add a splash of vinaigrette.*

INGREDIENTS

250 g/8 oz fusilli or other pasta	*2 spring onions, chopped*
6 asparagus spears	*50 g/2 oz walnut pieces*
3 tbsp extra-virgin olive oil	*90 g/3 oz green olives, pitted*
90 g/3 oz Parmesan cheese, plus extra for	*and quartered*
topping	*Salt and ground black pepper*
½ small courgette, thinly sliced	

Cook pasta according to the directions on the packet. While the pasta is cooking, blanch the asparagus for 2 to 3 minutes in boiling water. Drain and cut into 2.5-cm/1-in pieces.

When the pasta is cooked, drain but do not rinse, then put it in a large mixing bowl. Pour the olive oil over the pasta, and toss with two forks. Add the Parmesan, and toss again. Stir in the asparagus, courgettes, spring onions, walnuts and green olives. Add salt and pepper to taste. Serve with a sprinkling of Parmesan over the top.

SPAGHETTI WITH BROCCOLI AND PISTOU

Serves 4

Broccoli cooked with garlic, tomatoes and olive oil is tossed with spaghetti, then served with a generous scoop of pistou – a delicious mixture of crushed basil, garlic and olive oil, a French version of Italy's pesto. It is a deliciously hearty dish from the Italian region of Liguria.

INGREDIENTS

1 bunch broccoli, cut into bite-sized
pieces and florets

3–4 garlic cloves, chopped

4–5 tbsp extra-virgin olive oil

Pinch of crushed, dried red chilli pepper

400 g/14 oz canned tomatoes with
the juice, or fresh tomatoes

1 tbsp tomato purée, if using fresh
tomatoes

Sea salt to taste

375 g/12 oz spaghetti

3–5 tbsp pistou

Blanch the broccoli until tender but still crisp, then drain and place in a frying pan with the garlic, olive oil and chilli over a medium-high heat. Cook for a minute or two, then add the tomatoes, tomato purée and sea salt and cook for a few minutes over a high heat.

Cook the spaghetti until *al dente*, then drain and toss with the hot broccoli and tomato sauce. Serve each portion with a generous scoop of pistou.

SPICY VEGETABLE DISHES

SPICY GREEN BEANS

Serves 3–4

Marinate these beans early in the day, and you'll have a spicy dish by dinner. These make an easy and convenient addition to a picnic.

INGREDIENTS

500 g/1 lb fresh green beans, topped and tailed

2 tbsp vegetable oil

2 tbsp white wine vinegar

1 tbsp freshly squeezed lemon juice

1 tsp Creole or English mustard

1 garlic clove, crushed

1 spring onion, chopped

1 tsp chilli-pepper flakes

$\frac{1}{4}$ tsp salt

Cook the green beans in boiling water until just tender, 3 to 4 minutes. Drain and plunge into cold water, then drain well again. In a glass dish, whisk together all the remaining ingredients. Add the beans and stir to coat thoroughly. Refrigerate for at least 3 hours. Serve chilled.

PAPRIKA POTATO SALAD

Serves 4

*This salad has a spicy Indian flavour. Perfect served either as an accompaniment to
a spiced main dish or a green salad.*

INGREDIENTS

500 g/1 lb potatoes

150 ml/¼ pt vegetable stock

1 red onion, halved and sliced

¼ tsp ground cumin

1 green chilli, chopped

¼ tsp ground turmeric

1 cardamom pod

1 tsp paprika

1 tomato, seeded and diced

1 tbsp chopped fresh parsley

Cut the potatoes into 2.5-cm/1-in cubes. Cook in boiling water for 10 minutes. Drain well and reserve.

Heat 3 tablespoons of the stock in a pan, add the onion and cook for 5 minutes until beginning to brown. Add the potatoes, cumin, chilli, turmeric, cardamom pod and paprika. Stir in the remaining stock and the tomato. Bring to the boil and cook for 5 minutes. Remove the cardamom pod, sprinkle with parsley and serve.

SPICED AUBERGINES

Serves 4

An Indian aubergine dish which is perfect with curry or a plain vegetable casserole.
It is also delicious cold as an appetizer.

INGREDIENTS

500 g/1 lb aubergines	1/2 tsp curry powder
175 g/6 oz potatoes	3 garlic cloves, crushed
4 tbsp vegetable stock	1 tsp chilli powder
1/2 onion, sliced	Pinch of ground turmeric
1 small red pepper, seeded and diced	Pinch of sugar
1/4 tsp ground coriander	1 green chilli, diced
1/4 tsp ground cumin	1 tbsp chopped fresh coriander
1 tsp finely chopped ginger	

Dice the aubergines into small cubes. Cut the potatoes into 2.5-cm/1-in chunks. Heat the stock in a pan, add the onion and cook for 2 to 3 minutes. Stir in the red pepper, ground coriander, cumin, ginger, curry powder, garlic, chilli powder and turmeric, and cook for 2 to 3 minutes.

Add the aubergines, sugar, green chilli and 150 ml/1/4 pt water, cover and simmer for 15 minutes. Add the potato, cover and cook for 10 minutes. Stir in the fresh coriander and serve.

HARISSA

Makes about 250 ml/8 fl oz

Harissa or 'arhissa', *as it is sometimes called, is a fiery paste based on chillies. It is primarily associated with Tunisia but it is also used in Algeria and Morocco. As well as being served as a condiment in a small dish, Harissa is also used in cooking to liven up meat, poultry or vegetable casseroles, saffron-flavoured fish soups and stews, cooked red peppers and tomatoes. It is often used as a base for poached eggs, or added to dips, sauces and salad dressings.*

INGREDIENTS

50 g/2 oz dried red chillies, soaked in hot water for 1 hour

2 garlic cloves, chopped

2 tsp coriander seeds

2 tsp cumin seeds

2 tsp caraway seeds

Pinch of salt

6 tbsp olive oil

Drain the chillies and put in a mortar, spice grinder or small blender with the garlic, spices and salt. Mix to a paste then stir in 3 tablespoons of olive oil. Transfer to a small jar and pour a little oil over the surface. Cover and keep in the refrigerator for up to two days.

SPICED POTATO CAKES

Serves 4–6

These tasty fried potato cakes come from Algeria. The spicy mashed potato
mixture is also good served as it is.

INGREDIENTS

1 kg/2 lb mashed potatoes

1 tbsp paprika

2 tsp ground cumin

Good pinch of cayenne pepper

1 bunch of coriander, chopped

3 eggs

Salt and ground black pepper

Oil for frying

In a large bowl, mix the potato with the spices, coriander, eggs and seasoning. With floured hands, form the mixture into round flat cakes. Cover and refrigerate for 30 minutes.

Heat a shallow layer of oil in a large frying pan, add the cakes in batches and fry until crisp and golden brown on both sides. Transfer to kitchen paper to absorb any excess oil. Serve hot.

SPICED PARSNIPS

Serves 4–6

This version of the Tunisian Mzoura *is sweet and spicy, and can be made as hot as you like by adding*
Harissa. *It is also made, more traditionally, with carrots.*

INGREDIENTS

1 kg/2 lb small parsnips, sliced	1 tsp ground coriander
3 tbsp olive oil	1 tsp clear honey
1 small onion, finely chopped	150 ml/¼ pt vegetable stock
1 garlic clove, finely chopped	Salt and ground black pepper
1 tsp Harissa (see page 107)	Chopped coriander, to garnish
1 tsp ground cumin	

Cook the parsnips in a saucepan of boiling water for about 7 minutes, then drain. Meanwhile, heat the oil in a frying pan, then add the onion and garlic and cook gently until softened. Stir in the *Harissa* and spices, then add the honey, stock, parsnips and seasoning. Cook for 7 to 10 minutes, until the parsnips are tender and the liquid reduced to a sauce. Serve hot or cold sprinkled with coriander.

Spiced Potato Cakes ▶

SPICED GLAZED CARROTS WITH DILL

Serves 4

Dill, ginger and orange give this dish its distinctive flavour. Shake the pan towards the end of cooking to prevent the carrots from sticking.

INGREDIENTS

500 g/1 lb carrots, cut into thin sticks

50 g/2 oz butter

1 tbsp sugar

1-cm/$\frac{1}{2}$-inch piece stem ginger, chopped

Thickly grated rind of 1 orange

Salt and ground black pepper

Few sprigs of dill, chopped

Put the carrots, butter, sugar, ginger, orange rind and seasoning in a pan and just cover with water. Bring to the boil then simmer for about 12 minutes until the carrots are tender and the liquid has evaporated. Garnish with dill.

FRIED PEPPERS WITH CAPERS AND GARLIC

Serves 4–6

The essential character of this dish comes from the slightly charred taste of the peppers, which are fried until their skins are scorched. Serve hot as a vegetable accompaniment or chilled as an appetizer.

INGREDIENTS

4 tbsp olive oil

840 g/1¾ lb red peppers, cut into strips

4 garlic cloves, sliced

1 tbsp salt-packed capers

2 tbsp white wine vinegar

Salt and ground black pepper

Heat the oil in a frying pan until it is quite hot, then fry the peppers, stirring frequently, until they are charred around the edges. Add the garlic and capers. Cook until they sizzle, then stir in the vinegar and seasoning; because of the salt in the capers little additional salt will be necessary.

Allow the vinegar to evaporate for a minute or so, then either serve immediately, or leave to cool, cover, chill and serve cold.

POLENTA WITH SALSA

Serves 6

This is a hybrid dish, combining Italian polenta with black-eyed bean salsa, a recipe from the American South. The polenta must be prepared in advance. Traditional polenta – a coarse grind of cornmeal – needs cooking for at least 30 minutes.

INGREDIENTS

Polenta (recipe follows)

Olive oil for frying or grilling

375 g/12 oz Cheddar cheese, thinly sliced

260 g/9 oz black-eyed bean salsa

(bought salsa mixed with beans)

INGREDIENTS FOR POLENTA

2 tsp salt

300 g/10 oz polenta

Lightly oil a loaf tin, about 22 x 13 cm/ 9 x 5 in. Bring 1 1/2 l/2¼ pt water and the salt to the boil in a large saucepan. Slowly add the polenta, stirring constantly and watching for lumps. Cook over a low heat, stirring almost constantly for 30 minutes or so, until the polenta forms a thick mass that pulls cleanly away from the sides of pan. Pour the polenta into the loaf tin and smooth the top. Let it cool for at least 30 minutes before turning out.

Cut the polenta into slices about 4 cm/1½ in thick. If you are going to barbecue it, lightly brush the cut edges with olive oil. If you are going to fry it, heat 1 tablespoon olive oil in a pan.

When the oil is hot, or when the barbecue coals are glowing and the flames have died, put the polenta slices on the heat. Cook until the bottom is golden (if frying) or charred with grid marks, about 3 minutes. Turn the polenta and put the sliced cheese on top. Cook until the underneath is golden or charred. (Note: If you are frying the polenta, the cheese will melt more readily if you use a lid on the pan. Add more oil if necessary before frying the next batch of polenta.)

Remove the polenta from the heat. Spoon black-eyed bean salsa over the top, and serve.

AUBERGINE AND POTATO CURRY

Serves 4

This makes a substantial main course, but it could also be served as a side dish with curries.

INGREDIENTS

2 tsp cumin seeds

1 tbsp mustard seeds

3 tbsp ghee or sunflower oil

2 small sweet potatoes, about 500 g/1 lb,

peeled and cut into 1-cm/

¹/₂-in chunks

1 large onion, finely sliced

2 garlic cloves, sliced

1–2 tsp chilli powder

1 tsp ground turmeric

1 large aubergine, cut the same size as

the potato

1 tbsp poppy seeds

300 ml/¹/₂ pt water or vegetable stock

2 tsp salt

1 tbsp torn fresh coriander leaves

Heat a large frying pan over a medium heat, then add the cumin and mustard seeds and quickly dry-fry for 30 seconds or so, until aromatic and starting to pop. Transfer to a plate and leave to cool.

Heat the ghee or oil in the pan, add the potatoes and cook for 3 to 4 minutes until starting to soften. Add the onion, garlic, chilli powder and turmeric, and cook for 1 to 2 minutes, then add the aubergines with the roasted spices and

the poppy seeds. Stir in the water and salt, then cover and simmer slowly for 30 to 45 minutes, until the vegetables are tender.

Season the curry to taste, then serve sprinkled with the coriander.

BARBECUED CORN

Serves 6

Corn on the cob is delicious barbecued. This recipe uses butter that has been seasoned with fresh chives and paprika, but you can substitute other fresh herbs and spices to suit your taste – basil, oregano, cumin, cayenne pepper and chilli powder all work well. Or brush the corn with garlic-flavoured olive oil.

INGREDIENTS

6 corn on the cob

125 g/4 oz butter, softened to room temperature

2 tbsp snipped fresh chives

1 tsp paprika

Mound a pyramid of coals in the centre of the barbecue, set alight and leave to heat up.

Rinse and wipe the corn dry. If the husks are on, don't remove them. If not, you can use foil instead.

Put the softened butter in a small bowl with the chives and paprika. Mash the butter with a fork until the chives and paprika are well mixed into it. Spread a scant amount of butter on each corn cob. You don't want to use more than half the butter on this step. If you do, make more seasoned butter to serve on the side. Pull the husks back up so all the corn is covered. If there are no husks or if they have been trimmed to expose part of the corn, wrap each cob in foil.

When the barbecue flames have died and the coals are glowing and covered with ash, put the corn around the edges of the grill, not over the coals. Cook the corn for 20–25 minutes. Turn several times during cooking, so that all sides are exposed to the heat. When the corn is cooked, quickly remove the husks or foil and roll the cobs around on the grill above the coals for just a minute or two, so they show spots of browning.

Serve the corn with the remaining seasoned butter on the side.

OKRA AND TOMATO TAGINE

Serves 4

Be sure to choose small okra. In North Africa, the okra are threaded on string, so they can be lifted out when the tagine (stew) is stirred. Serve as a main course or with grilled vegetables.

INGREDIENTS

500 g/1 lb fresh okra

3 tbsp olive oil

1 large onion, finely chopped

2 garlic cloves, finely chopped

Pinch of cayenne pepper

750 g/1½ lb well-flavoured tomatoes, peeled, seeded and chopped

Pinch of paprika

4 tbsp chopped fresh parsley

Salt and ground black pepper

Trim the stalks off the okra without cutting the pods. Heat the oil in a pan and fry the okra until lightly browned. Remove with a slotted spoon.

Add the onion and garlic to the pan and fry until soft but not browned. Stir in the paprika and cayenne pepper, stirring for 30 seconds, then add the tomatoes. Bring to the boil and simmer for 10 minutes. Add the okra, half the parsley, plenty of pepper and a little salt. Simmer, stirring occasionally, for about 30 minutes.

If the sauce is not well reduced, transfer the okra to a warm dish and keep warm. Boil the sauce until thickened. Pour over the okra. Serve warm or cold, sprinkled with the remaining parsley.

SWEETCORN SALSA

Makes about 375 ml/10 fl oz

Corn salsa is colourful and crunchy, and the jalapeños add a gentle heat. For a spicier salsa, don't trim the veins and the seeds from the jalapeños.

INGREDIENTS

250 g/8 oz sweetcorn	1 tbsp chopped fresh coriander
3 tbsp diced red pepper	2 tbsp olive oil
3 tbsp diced green pepper	2 tbsp fresh lime juice
2 jalapeño chillies, seeded and chopped	¼ tsp ground cumin
30 g/1 oz spring onions, chopped	¼ tsp salt
1 large tomato, seeded and chopped	Pinch of black pepper

Put the sweetcorn in a small saucepan with 3 tablespoons boiling water. Cook until just tender, about 7 minutes. Drain and leave to cool. Meanwhile, combine all the remaining ingredients. Stir in the corn. Let stand for about 15 minutes for the flavours to blend, then taste and adjust the seasoning.

MUSHROOMS IN WHITE WINE

Serves 4–6

This dish is wonderful made with wild mushrooms, but use cultivated ones if they are not available.
Serve with fried or toasted bread.

INGREDIENTS

1 large onion, finely chopped

4 tbsp olive oil

2 garlic cloves, finely chopped

½ chilli, seeded and chopped, or cayenne

pepper to taste

1 kg/2 lb mushrooms, preferably including

porcini (ceps), cleaned and sliced

Salt and ground black pepper

150 ml/¼ pt dry white wine

2 tbsp brandy

2 tbsp chopped fresh parsley

Fry the onion in the oil in a large flameproof casserole, adding the garlic and chilli or cayenne pepper once it has softened. Add the sliced mushrooms and fry until they soften. Season and add the wine and brandy. Cook to reduce the liquid a little, sprinkle with parsley and serve.

SLIGHTLY SPICY LEEKS

Serves 4

The combination of orange, leek and spice is delicious but if the orange clashes with your main dish it may be omitted or the rind of half a lemon added instead.

INGREDIENTS

4 tbsp oil

2 tbsp crushed coriander seeds

Grated rind and juice of 1 orange

¼ tsp allspice

500 g/1 lb leeks, sliced thin and separated into rings

Salt and ground black pepper

Heat the oil, then stir-fry the crushed coriander with the orange rind and allspice over a fairly low heat for 2 to 3 minutes, or until the orange rind is quite bright and the mixture is fragrant.

Toss in all the leeks and increase the heat, then stir-fry the vegetables for 8 minutes, or until they are softened. Add the orange juice and boil hard for 2 minutes, tossing the leeks to coat them in a spicy glaze. Taste and season, then serve at once.

SPICY RICE WITH WATERCRESS

Serves 4

This rice dish was designed as a stuffing, but you can also serve it as a side dish.
The almonds add crunch, and the watercress adds a subtle flavour.

INGREDIENTS

500 g/1 lb chopped watercress

2–4 tbsp vegetable oil

250 g/8 oz chopped onion

50 g/2 oz chopped celery

50 g/2 oz chopped green pepper

2 garlic cloves, crushed

300 ml/¹/₂ pt vegetable stock

¹/₄ tsp black pepper

¹/₄ tsp salt

¹/₄ tsp cayenne pepper

¹/₂ tsp dry mustard

¹/₄ tsp ground cumin

Slivered almonds, toasted (see note)

175 g/6 oz cooked rice

2 spring onions, chopped

Wash the watercress. Dry with kitchen paper or in a salad spinner. Chop coarsely. In a medium frying pan, sauté the watercress in 2 tablespoons oil until limp, 4 to 5 minutes. Remove from the pan and set aside.

Add oil to the pan if needed, and sauté the onion, celery, green pepper and garlic until they are tender, about 5 minutes. Add the vegetable stock and spices. Cook over a medium heat until the liquids are slightly reduced. Add the watercress, almonds, rice and spring onions. Stir well. Any excess stuffing can be cooked for 20 minutes, covered, in a lightly oiled casserole dish.

Note: to toast almonds, spread in a single layer on a baking sheet. Bake at 180°C/350°F/Gas 5 until lightly browned, 10 minutes.

SALADS

ASPARAGUS AND MUSHROOM SALAD

Serves 4

The combination of asparagus and mushrooms makes a sophisticated salad. Just be sure that you give the asparagus a head start on the vinaigrette: mushrooms are notorious sponges, and will soak up the dressing before the asparagus has a chance to absorb any of the flavour.

INGREDIENTS

750 g/1½ lb fresh asparagus	¼ tsp fresh thyme or a pinch of dried thyme
125 g/4 oz mushrooms	
2 tbsp white wine vinegar	¼ tsp fresh oregano or a pinch of dried oregano
125 ml/3½ fl oz olive oil	
¼ tsp Dijon mustard	¼ tsp salt
1 garlic clove, crushed	Pinch of ground black pepper
¼ tsp snipped fresh chives	

Snap the bottoms off the asparagus spears. Blanch for 3 to 5 minutes in boiling water, depending on the thickness of the spears. Drain and chill.

Prepare the vinaigrette by mixing all the remaining ingredients except the mushrooms. Shake well and pour over the asparagus.

After the asparagus has been in the vinaigrette for at least 20 minutes, clean, trim and slice the mushrooms. Add them to the salad and spoon some of the vinaigrette over them. Allow to marinate for at least a further 20 minutes.

AUBERGINE AND MINT SALAD

Serves 4–6

A creamy salad that can be spiced up a bit with toasted cumin seeds, fennel or coriander seeds.
This can also be served as an accompaniment to curries.

INGREDIENTS

1 tbsp cumin seeds

125 ml/3½ fl oz fruity olive oil

1 large aubergine, sliced

1 garlic clove, crushed

2 tbsp chopped fresh mint

300 ml/½ pt plain yoghurt

Salt and ground black pepper

Heat a large, ridged frying pan over a moderate heat, then add the cumin seeds and dry roast for 30 seconds, until fragrant and just starting to pop. Transfer to a saucer and leave until required.

Heat the oil in the pan, then add the aubergine slices and fry on both sides until lightly browned and tender. Do not be tempted to add more oil as some will run from the aubergine as it cooks. Remove the slices from the pan and leave to cool, then place them in a shallow dish, sprinkle with the cumin, garlic and mint and leave until cold.

Spoon on the yoghurt and season well. Serve lightly chilled.

SPINACH AND FIG SALAD

Serves 4

A low-calorie salad that looks exotic, yet it is surprisingly quick and simple to make.

INGREDIENTS

500 g/1 lb fresh spinach, washed

50 g/2 oz pine nuts

3 fresh figs

Dressing (recipe follows)

A few fresh nasturtium flowers (optional)

For the dressing

90 ml/3 fl oz olive oil

2 tbsp fresh lemon juice

Salt and ground black pepper

Remove and discard any coarse stems from the spinach and tear the leaves into pieces. Place in a colander to drain well. Place the pine nuts in a small, dry baking tin and roast until lightly browned, stirring all the time. Remove from the tin and leave to cool.

Wash the figs, trim off the stems and cut each into quarters then into thin slices. Place the spinach, pine nuts and figs into a serving bowl. Make the dressing. Sprinkle over the dressing, toss well and garnish with a few fresh nasturtium flowers, if available.

CUCUMBER SALAD

Serves 4

This salad benefits from a couple of hours marinating.

INGREDIENTS

2 large cucumbers, peeled and
thinly sliced

½ mild onion, thinly sliced

½ red pepper, cut into
julienne strips

For the dressing

90 ml/3 fl oz olive oil

2 tbsp fresh lemon juice

1 garlic clove, crushed

2 tsp chopped fresh parsley

1 tsp chopped fresh tarragon

¼ tsp salt

Ground black pepper

Put the cucumber, onion and pepper in bowl. Make the dressing by combining the remaining ingredients, then whisk or shake well. Pour the dressing over the salad.

TOMATO SALAD WITH OLIVE SALSA

Serves 4

This simple salad depends on excellent ingredients – perfectly ripe tomatoes, preferably fresh,
mozzarella cheese and fresh basil leaves. Top it with salsa for a luscious summer dish.

INGREDIENTS

4 large, ripe tomatoes

Several sprigs of fresh basil

125 g/4 oz fresh mozzarella cheese

About 300 ml/¹⁄₂ pt salsa mixed with

fresh, pitted olives

Core the tomatoes and slice thickly. Arrange the slices on four salad plates. Rinse the basil, pull off the leaves and dry them on kitchen paper. Arrange the basil leaves on top of the tomato slices. Cut the mozzarella into thin slices and place on top of the tomato and basil. Then spoon the salsa over the tomatoes and cheese.

JICAMA–ORANGE SALAD

Serves 4–6

This refreshing salad combines the crunch of fresh jicama, the tang of oranges, the bite of onion
and the fire of the jalapeño chilli. It is served with a slightly sweet dressing for an unusual flavour.

INGREDIENTS

3 medium oranges

¹⁄₂ medium red onion

175 g/6 oz peeled jicama (yam bean), cut

into 1-cm/¹⁄₂-inch cubes

Dressing (recipe follows)

Lettuce leaves

For the dressing

6 tbsp olive oil

3 tbsp red wine vinegar

2 tbsp orange juice

2 tsp honey

¹⁄₄ tsp chilli powder

1 jalapeño chile, unseeded, finely chopped

Peel the oranges and slice them thinly, removing the seeds. Thinly slice the onion, then separate the slices into rings. Mix the orange, onion and jicama together, toss with the dressing and serve over lettuce.

Combine all the dressing ingredients in a bottle and shake well to mix.

Tomato Salad with Olive Salsa ▶

BEANSPROUT SALAD

Serves 4

A light, crisp salad that makes an excellent appetizer or side dish.

INGREDIENTS

500 g/1 lb beansprouts

1 tsp salt

1¼ l/4 pt water

2 tbsp light soy sauce

1 tbsp white wine vinegar

2 tbsp sesame oil

2 spring onions, finely chopped

Wash and rinse the beansprouts in cold water discarding the husks and other bits and pieces that float to the surface. It is not necessary to trim each sprout. Blanch in a pan of salted, boiling water. Pour into a colander and rinse in cold water until cool. Drain.

Place the beansprouts in a bowl or a deep dish and add the soy sauce, vinegar and sesame oil. Toss well and garnish with spring onions just before serving.

AUBERGINE, FENNEL AND WALNUT SALAD

Serves 6

The delicate, aniseed flavour of the fennel and the crunch of the nuts contrast well with the aubergine.

INGREDIENTS

175 ml/6 fl oz olive oil

1 bulb fennel, thinly sliced, feathery
leaves reserved for garnish

1 small red onion, sliced

175 g/6 oz walnut pieces

Sea salt and ground black pepper

1 aubergine, cut into 1-cm/½-in pieces

1 tbsp red wine vinegar

1 tomato, skinned, seeded and chopped

1 tbsp torn fresh basil leaves

Fennel leaves and basil sprigs, to garnish

Heat 3 tablespoons of olive oil in a frying pan and add the fennel and onion. Cook until just soft but not browned, about 5 to 8 minutes. Remove with a slotted spoon and place in a bowl.

Add 2 tablespoons of oil to the pan, then stir in the walnut pieces and fry them for about 2 minutes, until crisp and browned but not burnt. Remove the nuts from the pan with a slotted spoon and drain on kitchen paper. Place the nuts in a bowl, sprinkle with salt and toss until well coated and cool.

Add 4 tablespoons of oil to the pan, then add the aubergines and fry over a medium heat until tender and browned on all sides. Remove from the pan and add to the fennel and onion. Add the remaining oil to the pan with the red wine vinegar and a little salt and pepper. Heat, stirring, until the dressing is simmering, then pour over the vegetables in the bowl. Toss lightly, then leave to cool for 10 to 15 minutes.

When the salad is still slightly warm, add the walnuts, chopped tomato and basil. Leave until cold, then serve garnished with fennel leaves and basil sprigs.

MEDITERRANEAN SALAD

Serves 4

Any combination of vegetables would be delicious steeped in this tomato and garlic sauce.
Be sure to chill the dish well and serve with crusty bread to mop up the juices.

INGREDIENTS

300 ml/½ pt vegetable stock

1 onion, finely chopped

1 garlic clove, crushed

60 ml/2 fl oz dry white wine

4 tomatoes, peeled and chopped

Juice of 1 lime

1 tbsp cider vinegar

2 tsp tomato purée

1 tsp fennel seeds

1 tsp mustard seeds

75 g/3 oz button mushrooms, quartered

2 oz French beans, trimmed

1 courgette, sliced

Ground black pepper

Basil leaves, to garnish

Heat the stock in a large saucepan and cook the onion and garlic for 3 to 4 minutes. Add the wine, tomatoes, lime juice, vinegar, tomato purée, fennel and mustard seeds and the vegetables. Bring the mixture to the boil, reduce the heat and simmer for 20 minutes or until the vegetables are just cooked. Season to taste with black pepper.

Transfer the mixture to a serving dish, cover and chill for at least 1 hour. Garnish with basil and serve.

WARM MUSHROOM SALAD

Serves 4

If liked, add a handful of chopped, toasted hazelnuts
to this simple but delicious bistro-style salad.

INGREDIENTS

375 g/12 oz small thin asparagus, tough
ends broken off

3 shallots, chopped

2 garlic cloves, chopped

4 tbsp olive oil

180 g/7 oz mixed salad leaves

Salt and ground black pepper

1 tbsp tarragon mustard

1 tbsp raspberry or red wine vinegar

125 g/4 oz goat's cheese, crumbled

375 g/12 oz mixed fresh mushrooms, such
as oyster, porcini (ceps) and button, cut
into strips or bite-sized pieces

1 tbsp balsamic vinegar

Handful of fresh chervil, chopped

2 tbsp snipped fresh chives or chopped
fresh tarragon

Cook the asparagus in rapidly boiling salted water until just tender and bright green, about 3 minutes. Drain, plunge into very cold or iced water to keep its bright green colour and crisp texture, then drain once again. Set the asparagus aside while you prepare the rest of the salad.

Mix 1 tablespoon of the chopped shallots with half the garlic and 1 to 2 tablespoons olive oil. Toss with the salad leaves, along with salt and pepper to taste. Mix 1 tablespoon olive oil with the tarragon mustard and the raspberry or red wine vinegar; stir well to combine, then pour it over the leaves and toss well. Arrange the asparagus and goat's cheese over the top.

Sauté the mushrooms over a medium-high heat, with the remaining shallots and garlic, in the remaining olive oil until lightly browned. Pour in the balsamic vinegar, season with salt and pepper then pour this hot mixture over the salad. Serve immediately, with the herbs scattered over.

ANDALUCIAN CHOPPED VEGETABLE SALAD

Serves 4

Served chilled, this exquisitely refreshing salad is perfect in hot weather.

INGREDIENTS

1 large cucumber, diced

3–5 small, ripe tomatoes, diced

1 carrot, diced

1 red pepper, diced

1 green pepper, diced (add a yellow or

orange pepper here, too, if desired)

3–5 spring onions, thinly sliced, or 1 small

onion, chopped

3–5 garlic cloves, crushed

¼ tsp ground cumin or cumin seeds

Salt

Juice of 1 lemon

1 tsp sherry vinegar or white wine vinegar

3 tbsp extra-virgin olive oil or to taste

Combine the cucumber, tomatoes, carrot, red and green peppers, spring onions and garlic. Toss with cumin, salt, lemon, sherry or white wine vinegar, olive oil and herbs. Taste for seasoning, and chill until ready to serve.

EGYPTIAN VEGETABLE SALAD

Serves 4

Ful medames are beans which are used widely in Egyptian cuisine. They are often simply served drizzled with olive oil with a salad garnish. Here they are used in a salad. Serve with warm pitta bread.

INGREDIENTS

375 g/12 oz cooked ful medames or

borlotti beans

2–3 hard-boiled eggs, preferably still

warm, peeled and diced

Extra-virgin olive oil, as desired

3–4 garlic cloves, crushed

Large pinch of salt

1 onion, chopped

Handful of rocket, coarsely chopped

2–3 ripe tomatoes, chopped

1 tbsp each: coriander, dill, mint

2 lemons, cut into wedges

Warm the beans in their juices, then drain and arrange on a platter. Garnish with the eggs.

Work several tablespoons of the olive oil into the garlic, then pour this over the beans. Season and sprinkle the onion, rocket, tomatoes, coriander, dill and mint around the top, and garnish with lemon. Drizzle extra olive oil over the top, and serve with a small jug of olive oil and a bowl of coarse sea salt for sprinkling.

◄ *Andalucian Chopped Vegetable Salad*

FATTOUSH

Serves 4

This Lebanese salad of bread and salad vegetables, characteristically dressed with lots of olive oil and lemon, is very refreshing. Serve it with plain yoghurt, or yoghurt mixed with feta cheese.

INGREDIENTS

1 large or 2 small cucumbers, diced	*3 garlic cloves, chopped*
3 ripe tomatoes, diced	*125 ml/4 fl oz extra-virgin olive oil*
1 green pepper, diced	*Juice of 3 lemons*
8 tbsp each: chopped fresh mint, coriander, parsley	*3–4 pitta breads, stale and lightly toasted, then broken into pieces*
3 spring onions, thinly sliced	
1 tsp salt	

Combine the cucumbers, tomatoes, pepper, mint, coriander, parsley, spring onions, salt, garlic, olive oil and lemon juice. Chill for at least 1 hour. Just before serving, toss with the broken pitta bread.

BULGUR, RED PEPPER, CUCUMBER AND CHEESE SALAD

Serves 4–6

Black olives in oil can also be added to this salad just before serving, if you like.

INGREDIENTS

375 g/12 oz bulgur wheat

300 ml/½ pt boiling water

4 tbsp olive oil

3 tbsp lemon juice

3 tbsp chopped fresh coriander

2 tbsp chopped fresh mint

Salt and ground black pepper

1 red pepper, grilled, skinned and sliced

1 bunch of plump spring onions, chopped

2 garlic cloves, chopped

½ cucumber, coarsely chopped

175 g/6 oz crumbled feta cheese

Lime wedges, to serve

Place the bulgur wheat in a large bowl, add the boiling water, and leave to soak for 30 minutes, stirring occasionally with a fork, until the water has been absorbed.

In a mixing bowl, whisk together the oil, lemon juice and seasoning. Pour the oil mixture over the bulgur wheat, add the herbs and mix well. Then mix in the remaining ingredients. Cover and chill until required. Serve garnished with lime wedges and olives, if you like.

ROASTED PUMPKIN SALAD

Serves 4

Serve this salad warm or cold, on a bed of rocket leaves if you wish, with plenty of bread to mop up the delicious juices. You could add a few shavings of Parmesan cheese, if you like.

INGREDIENTS

8 slices from a small pumpkin, each about

2 cm/¾ in thick, seeded

1 aubergine, quartered lengthwise

2 large slicing tomatoes, halved

6–8 large garlic cloves, unpeeled

Salt and ground black pepper

6–8 basil leaves, torn in half

Sugar

Italian bread (eg ciabatta), to serve

For the dressing

6 tbsp extra-virgin olive oil

1 tbsp balsamic or sherry vinegar

1 tsp Dijon mustard

Salt and ground black pepper

Pinch of sugar

1 tsp chopped fresh young lovage

leaves or 1 tbsp chopped fresh

flat-leaf parsley

Preheat the oven to 220°C/425°F/Gas 7. Arrange the prepared vegetables with the garlic in a roasting tin, then season with salt and pepper. Push the basil leaves into the flesh of the tomatoes, then scatter over a little sugar. Drizzle everything with olive oil, then roast at the top of the oven for 40 to 45 minutes, until the vegetables are just starting to blacken. (Check after 30 minutes and remove the tomatoes if they are already soft.)

Allow the vegetables to cool slightly, then cut the pumpkin away from the skin. Leave the vegetables for 10 minutes, if you intend to serve the salad warm, or until completely cold.

Prepare the dressing by blending all the ingredients together and season with salt, pepper and sugar to taste. Peel the garlic, then arrange the vegetables on four serving plates. Pour the dressing over and add a little fresh basil to each helping. Serve immediately with plenty of olive oil bread.

ROASTED SQUASH, VEGETABLE AND PASTA SALAD

Serves 4

Enjoy this filling salad as a main course or reduce the quantities and serve as an appetizer.

INGREDIENTS

4 x 2.5-cm/1-in slices squash, seeded

2 courgettes, trimmed

1 large aubergine, halved lengthwise

1 large red pepper

1 bulb garlic

Salt and ground black pepper

Olive oil

7 oz fresh or dried tagliatelle, spaghetti, or other noodles

For the dressing

6 tbsp extra-virgin olive oil

2 tbsp balsamic vinegar

1 tsp Dijon mustard

Sugar

Mixed salad leaves, to serve

Salt and ground black pepper

Preheat the oven to 220°C/425°F/Gas 7. Place all the vegetables and the garlic in a roasting tin, season lightly and drizzle with olive oil. Roast for 40 minutes, or until tender and beginning to blacken. Turn the courgette, pepper and aubergine during cooking, and remove the vegetables as they are done.

Cover the pepper with a clean damp cloth as soon as it comes out of the oven, then leave all the vegetables to cool. Peel the skin away from the pepper as soon as it is cool enough to handle, then remove the core and seed.

Blend all the ingredients for the dressing together. Cook the pasta in plenty of boiling salted water until *al dente*. Drain in a colander and shake briefly, then turn into a serving dish and add half the vinaigrette. Toss briefly, then leave to cool.

Peel the squash, chop the roasted vegetables into bite-sized pieces and squeeze the garlic cloves from their skins. Pile the vegetables over the pasta, then top with the salad leaves. Pour over the remaining dressing, then serve.

SIDE DISHES AND ACCOMPANIMENTS

ORIENTAL BEANSPROUTS

Serves 4

Beansprouts are the main ingredient for a chop suey. The combination of vegetables may be changed to suit the season or the ingredients you have to hand.

INGREDIENTS

2 tsp cornflour

2 tbsp soy sauce

1 tbsp dry sherry

2 tbsp oil

1 tsp sesame oil

1 celery stalk, cut into fine short strips

1 green pepper, seeded and cut into fine short strips

½ onion, thinly sliced

375 g/12 oz beansprouts

Blend the cornflour with the soy sauce, sherry and 2 tablespoons of water; set aside.

Heat both oils together, then stir-fry the celery, pepper and onion for 5 minutes. The vegetables should be lightly cooked and still crunchy. Toss in the beansprouts and stir-fry for 1 minute. Give the cornflour mixture a stir, pour it into the pan, and bring the juices to the boil, stirring all the time. Cook for 2 minutes, stirring, then serve at once.

FRENCH BEANS AND NEW POTATOES IN PESTO

Serves 4

Although this dish takes advantage of the bounty of the summer garden, it can be made with potatoes and beans that are available year-round, and pesto that is made in quantity during the summer, and frozen in small batches.

INGREDIENTS

500 g/1 lb tiny new potatoes, washed and cut in half	*Handful of fresh basil leaves*
500 g/1 lb French beans, washed and trimmed	*150 g/5 oz Parmesan or pecorino cheese, grated*
2 tbsp pine nuts or chopped walnuts	*90 ml/3 fl oz olive oil*
1 garlic clove, peeled	*¼ tsp salt*
	Pinch of ground black pepper

Boil the potatoes for 10 minutes. Boil the French beans until tender, 3 to 4 minutes. While the potatoes and beans are cooking, put the remaining ingredients in a food processor and process for 10 seconds, until the basil is chopped but the mixture is not turned into a paste.

Drain the potatoes and beans. Toss with the pesto.

COUSCOUS WITH DRIED APRICOTS AND ALMONDS

Serves 8

INGREDIENTS

375 g/12 oz pre-cooked couscous

90 g/3 oz ready-to-eat dried apricots, sliced into strips

Salt and ground black pepper

50 g/2 oz blanched almonds, toasted

Chopped fresh coriander, to serve

Butter or olive oil, to serve (optional)

Put the couscous in a bowl and pour over 600 ml/1 pt water. Leave for about 30 minutes or until most of the water has been absorbed; stir frequently with a fork to keep the grains separate. Stir the apricots and seasoning into the couscous then tip into a steamer or metal colander lined with muslin. Place over a saucepan of boiling water, cover tightly with foil and steam for about 20 minutes until hot. Stir in the almonds, coriander and butter or oil, if using.

TRIO OF PUREES

Serves 4

INGREDIENTS

300 g/10 oz potatoes, cubed

250 g/8 oz carrots, cubed

Grated rind of 1 orange

1 tbsp orange juice

Ground black pepper

250 g/8 oz sweet potato, cubed

Pinch of grated nutmeg

125 g/4 oz spinach

Grated rind of 1 lemon

1 tbsp chopped fresh coriander

Cook the potatoes in boiling water for 20 minutes until soft. Drain and mash. Divide equally into three separate bowls. Boil the carrots for 10 minutes until soft. Drain and mash. Add to one bowl of potato with the orange rind and juice. Season with pepper.

Cook the sweet potato for 10 minutes in boiling water. Drain and mash. Add to another bowl of potato with the nutmeg. Season with pepper.

Blanch the spinach for 3 minutes in boiling water. Drain thoroughly. Add to the remaining bowl with the lemon rind and coriander. Season with pepper.

Place the contents of each bowl, separately, in a food processor and blend each for 1 minute each. Spoon one quarter of the carrot purée into the base of four lightly greased ramekin dishes. Top with one quarter of the spinach mixture and spoon over one quarter of the sweet potato mixture.

Place the dishes in a roasting tin and fill with enough boiling water to come halfway up the sides. Cover and cook at 190°C/375°F/Gas 5 for 1 hour. Remove from the roasting tin. Turn out the purées onto serving plates. Serve with a main vegetable dish.

Coucous with Dried Apricots and Almonds ▶

HERBED CAULIFLOWER

Serves 4

Cauliflower cheese traditionally has a rich cheese sauce coating the cauliflower.
This low-fat version uses a wine and herb sauce which is equally delicious.

INGREDIENTS

4 baby cauliflowers	300 ml/½ pt milk
2 mint sprigs	150 ml/¼ pt dry white wine
900 ml/1½ pt vegetable stock	2 tbsp cornflour
50 g/2 oz grated cheese	1 tbsp chopped fresh parsley
	1 tbsp chopped fresh coriander
For the sauce	1 tbsp chopped fresh thyme
150 ml/¼ pt vegetable stock	Ground black pepper

Trim the cauliflowers and place in a large pan with the mint and stock. Cook gently for 10 minutes. Meanwhile, place the stock for the sauce, the milk and white wine in a pan. Blend the cornflour with 4 tablespoons of cold water and add to the pan. Bring to the boil, stirring, and add the herbs. Season and simmer for 2 to 3 minutes.

Drain the cauliflower and place in an ovenproof dish. Pour on the sauce and top with the cheese. Grill for 2 to 3 minutes until the cheese has melted. Serve immediately.

MINTED BEANS AND CUCUMBER

Serves 4

Cucumber is not usually served hot, but it is cooked perfectly with the beans in this recipe and delicately flavoured with mint. An unusual but delicious side dish.

INGREDIENTS

500 g/1 lb French beans, trimmed

½ cucumber, thickly sliced

2 garlic cloves, crushed

4 mint sprigs

1 tbsp lemon juice

90 ml/3 fl oz vegetable stock

Ground black pepper

Strips of lemon rind, to garnish

Place the vegetables on a large sheet of foil. Bring up the sides of the foil around the vegetables and crimp to form an open package. Add the remaining ingredients, season and seal the top of the package.

Place the package in a steamer and cook for 25 minutes or until the beans are tender. Garnish and serve.

POTATOES AND SPINACH

Serves 4

This is delicious, especially if a bunch of fresh fenugreek leaves is added to it. These leaves are called methi *and can be obtained from most Asian grocers all year round. If you find some, use the leaves only and substitute these for 50 g/2 oz of the spinach.*

INGREDIENTS

400 g/14 oz fresh or frozen leaf spinach	60 g/2½ oz tomato, chopped
250 g/8 oz potatoes	¼ tsp turmeric
2 tbsp oil	½ tsp chilli powder
¼ tsp fenugreek seeds	Salt to taste
½ tsp cumin seeds	

If you are using fresh spinach, weigh it after you have removed the stalks and chopped it. Wash it thoroughly to remove all the hidden grit and leave it to drain in a colander. If you are using frozen spinach, defrost it and let it drain well in a colander.

Scrub the potatoes well and do not peel them. Cut the potatoes into quarters, then cut each quarter into 2 or more pieces, making 8 to 12 pieces from each potato. Heat the oil in a medium-sized heavy pan and fry the fenugreek and cumin seeds. As the seeds begin to sizzle, add the tomato, turmeric, chilli powder and salt. Mix and cook the mixture for half a minute. Add the spinach and potato, and mix thoroughly so that the vegetables are well coated in the spices.

Cover the pan and simmer for 15 to 20 minutes. If there is still a little moisture left after this time, remove the lid and dry it out a little by cooking rapidly over a medium to high heat for a further few minutes, taking care not to let it burn.

PUMPKIN WITH LEEKS

Serves 4

Stir-frying is one of the best cooking methods for pumpkin – the vegetable remains whole but slightly tender.

INGREDIENTS

2 tbsp oil

Knob of butter

1 garlic clove, crushed

2 leeks, sliced

2 tsp ground cinnamon

50 g/2 oz sultanas

500 g/1 lb pumpkin, seeded and cubed

Salt and ground black pepper

Heat the oil and butter until the butter melts, then add the garlic, leeks, cinnamon and sultanas. Stir-fry the leeks for 5 minutes until they are softened and tender.

Add the pumpkin and seasoning. Continue stir-frying until the cubes are tender, but not soft enough to become mushy, which takes about 7 to 10 minutes. Serve the dish at once.

SWEET RED CABBAGE

Serves 4

Colourful and with a sweet-and-sour flavour, this dish may also be served cold.

INGREDIENTS

300 ml/½ pt vegetable stock

750 g/1½ lb red cabbage, shredded

1 onion, sliced

1 tbsp granulated brown sugar

1 tsp ground allspice

250 g/8 oz green apples, cored and sliced

1 tsp fennel seeds

2 tbsp cider vinegar

1 tbsp cornflour

1 tbsp chopped fresh parsley

Place half the stock in a large saucepan. Add the cabbage and onion and cook over a high heat for 5 minutes. Add the sugar, allspice, apples, fennel seeds, vinegar and remaining stock. Blend the cornflour with 2 tablespoons of cold water to form a paste. Stir into the pan and bring to the boil, stirring until thickened and clear.

Reduce the heat and cook for 15 minutes more until the cabbage is cooked. Sprinkle with the parsley and serve immediately.

CARAMELIZED BAKED ONIONS

Serves 4

These baked onions have a slightly 'burnt' taste which complements the sweetness of the onion.
Serve with a simple main dish.

INGREDIENTS

4 large onions

2 tsp polyunsaturated margarine

5 tbsp granulated brown sugar

Cut the onions into quarters and then into four again. Cook in boiling water for 10 minutes. Drain well.

Place the margarine and sugar in a pan and heat gently until melted.

Place the onions in a roasting tin and pour over the margarine and sugar. Cook in the oven at 190°C/375°F/Gas 5 for 10 minutes until browned. Serve immediately.

Sweet Red Cabbage ▶

THREE-MUSHROOM FRY

Serves 4

A simple but delicious dish. Three varieties of mushroom are cooked in garlic and soy sauce.

INGREDIENTS

90 g/3 oz open cap mushrooms

90 g/3 oz oyster mushrooms

90 g/3 oz shiitake mushrooms

4 tbsp vegetable stock

2 garlic cloves, crushed

1 tbsp soy sauce

2 tbsp chopped fresh parsley or thyme

Ground black pepper

Peel the open cap mushrooms and slice thinly. Place all the mushrooms in a pan with the stock, garlic, soy sauce and half the herbs. Season well with black pepper. Cook, stirring, for 3 to 4 minutes. Sprinkle in the remaining herbs and serve immediately.

CAULIFLOWER AND POTATO CURRY

Serves 2–3

A classic Indian side dish.

INGREDIENTS

6 tbsp oil

500 g/1 lb potatoes, peeled and quartered

1 small cauliflower, cut into large florets

³⁄₄ tsp ground turmeric

¹⁄₂ tsp chilli powder

1¹⁄₂ tsp ground cumin

³⁄₄ tsp salt

Large pinch of sugar

2 tomatoes, chopped

2 tsp ghee

¹⁄₂ tsp garam masala

Heat the oil in a large pan or wok over a medium high heat. Fry the potatoes a few pieces at a time until slightly brown. Remove and set aside. Fry the cauliflower pieces a few at a time until brown spots appear on them. Remove and set aside.

Lower the heat to medium, and add the turmeric, chilli, cumin, salt and sugar. Mix the spices together, add the tomatoes, and fry for 1 minute with the spices. Add 300 ml/¹⁄₂ pt of water and bring to the boil. Put in the potatoes, cover and cook for 10 minutes. Add the cauliflower, cover again and cook for a further 5 to 7 minutes until the potatoes and cauliflower are tender. Add the ghee and sprinkle with the garam masala. Remove from the heat and serve hot with rice and red lentils.

◀ *Three-Mushroom Fry*

BEETROOT WITH HORSERADISH

Serves 4

This flavourful side dish could also be served with blinis (Russian pancakes).

INGREDIENTS

4 tbsp oil

2 onions, halved and thinly sliced

500 g/1 lb cooked beetroot,
cut in small cubes

Salt and ground black pepper

3 tbsp chopped fresh dill

4 tbsp horseradish sauce

125 ml/4 fl oz soured cream

Heat the oil and stir-fry the onions for 10 minutes, until they are quite well cooked and beginning to brown. Add the beetroot with seasoning and continue to stir-fry for about 5 minutes for the beetroot to become hot, and for the flavour of the onions to mingle with it. Stir in the dill and transfer to a dish.

Mix the horseradish sauce with the soured cream and trickle this over the beetroot. Serve at once, tossing the horseradish cream with the beetroot and onion as the vegetables are spooned out.

CORIANDER POTATOES

Serves 4

Coriander works wonders for new potatoes, complementing their sweet fresh flavour perfectly.

INGREDIENTS

*1 kg/2 lb small new potatoes, scrubbed
and boiled*

Salt and ground black pepper

2 tsp caster sugar

2 tbsp lemon juice

4 tbsp olive oil

3 tbsp crushed coriander seeds

Strip of lemon rind

4 tbsp snipped chives

Cook the potatoes in boiling, slightly salted water for 10 to 15 minutes, or until tender. Drain. Stir the sugar and lemon juice together until the sugar dissolves completely.

Heat the oil and stir-fry the coriander for 2 minutes. Add the lemon rind and continue to cook for a further minute, pressing the piece of rind to bring out its flavour. Tip the potatoes into the pan and then stir-fry them for about 10 minutes, or until they are just beginning to brown on the outside.

Pour the sweetened lemon juice over the potatoes and mix them well with the oil in the pan, so that the liquids mingle to form a hot dressing. Mix in the chives, check the seasoning and serve at once.

MIXED VEGETABLE BHAJI

Serves 4

This mixture of vegetables has a new taste every time it is cooked, as the balance of ingredients seems to change.

INGREDIENTS

125 g/4 oz French beans	125 g/4 oz tomatoes	½ tsp chilli powder
175 g/6 oz potatoes	1–2 green chillies	¼ tsp turmeric powder
125 g/4 oz carrots	2 tbsp oil	½–¾ tsp salt
175 g/6 oz aubergines	7–8 garlic cloves, finely chopped	2–3 tbsp mint or coriander leaves

Top and tail the beans, then chop them into bite-sized lengths. Cut the potatoes into quarters and halve again. Scrape and dice the carrots. Cut the aubergine lengthwise into 4 strips and then slice across into 1-cm/½-in chunks. Chop the tomatoes and green chillies.

Measure the oil into a heavy pan over a medium heat. Add the garlic, stirring it as soon as it begins to turn translucent, then add all the vegetables. Also stir in the chilli powder, turmeric and salt. Mix the spices together. Lower the heat, cover the pan and cook for 20 to 25 minutes.

Add the mint or coriander leaves. Leave to stand for 2 to 3 minutes before serving.

HOT SPICY LENTILS

Serves 4

Red lentils provide the basis for a substantial side dish which is highly flavoured with spices and red chilli.

INGREDIENTS

175 g/6 oz red lentils	¼ tsp ground coriander
4 tsp polyunsaturated oil	1 red chilli, chopped
1 red onion, chopped	900 ml/1½ pt vegetable stock
2 garlic cloves, crushed	Juice and grated rind of 1 lime
¼ tsp ground cumin	Ground black pepper

Wash the lentils in 2 to 3 changes of water. Drain and reserve. Heat the oil in a pan, add the onion, garlic and spices and cook for 5 minutes. Stir in the lentils and cook for 3 to 4 minutes more.

Add the chilli and stock, and bring to the boil. Reduce the heat and simmer gently for 35 minutes until the lentils are soft. Stir in the lime juice and rind. Season well and serve.

◀ *Mixed Vegetable Bhaji*

DELICIOUS DESSERTS

HONEYED ORANGES

Serves 4

Oranges and ginger make a great combination. Ground ginger has been added to this recipe with a dash of orange liqueur for extra flavour.

INGREDIENTS

4 tbsp honey

½ tsp ground cinnamon

¼ tsp ground ginger

2 mint sprigs

2 tsp Grand Marnier

4 oranges

Place the honey, cinnamon, ginger and mint in a pan with 150 ml/¼ pt water. Heat gently to melt the honey. Bring to the boil and boil for 3 minutes to reduce by half. Remove the mint from the pan and discard. Stir in the Grand Marnier

Meanwhile, peel the oranges, remove the pith and slice thinly. Place the orange slices in a serving bowl, pour over the syrup and chill for 1 hour before serving.

STRAWBERRY FOOL

Serves 4

This dish is simple to prepare, but should be made in advance as it requires chilling for 1 hour before serving.

INGREDIENTS

300 g/10 oz strawberries, hulled and chopped

250 g/8 oz icing sugar

300 ml/½ pt plain yoghurt

2 egg whites

Strawberry slices and mint sprigs, to decorate

Place the chopped strawberries in a food processor with the icing sugar. Blend for 30 seconds until smooth.

Place the yoghurt in a bowl and stir in the strawberry mixture. Whisk the egg whites until peaks form and fold in gently. Spoon into serving glasses and chill for 1 hour. Decorate and serve.

Honeyed Oranges ▶

MELON ICE

Serves 4

*Any melon is suitable for this recipe. Colourful and refreshing,
it is the perfect light end to any meal.*

INGREDIENTS

125 g/4 oz sugar

3 mint sprigs

1 lb melon, such as cantaloupe, galia or
watermelon, seeded and diced

Mint, to decorate

Set the freezer to rapid-freeze. Place the sugar in a pan with 125 ml/4 fl oz water. Add the mint and cook over a gentle heat until the sugar dissolves. Remove the pan from the heat and strain the syrup. Discard the mint sprigs. Stir in 300 ml/½ pt of cold water.

Place the melon in a food processor and purée for 30 seconds until smooth. Stir into the syrup. Mix well and cool.

Place the mixture in a freezerproof container and freeze for 1 hour.

Remove from the freezer, pour the melon mixture into a bowl and whisk until smooth. Return to a clean freezerproof container and freeze for a further 30 minutes. Repeat the whisking process every 30 minutes for 2½ hours. Scoop into dishes, decorate with mint and serve immediately.

APRICOT SORBET

Serves 4

*Traditionally sorbets are served halfway through a meal to cleanse the palate,
but they are equally welcome at the end.*

INGREDIENTS

175 g/6 oz sugar

Juice of ½ orange

500 g/1 lb apricots, pitted and chopped

1 egg white

2 tbsp caster sugar

Apricot slices, mint sprigs and orange
rind, to decorate

Set the freezer to rapid-freeze. Place the sugar and orange juice in a pan with 150 ml/¼ pt water. Cook over a gentle heat to dissolve. Add a further 300 ml/½ pt water to the pan. Place the apricots in a food processor and purée for 30 seconds until smooth. Stir the apricot purée into the sugar syrup, place in a freezerproof container and freeze for 1 hour until half frozen. Whisk the egg white in a clean bowl until soft peaks

form and whisk in the sugar.

Turn the half-frozen fruit mixture into a bowl and whisk until smooth. Fold in the egg white and return to a freezerproof container. Freeze for 45 minutes. Turn the mixture out into a bowl, whisk again and return to a clean freezerproof container. Freeze for a further 2 hours until solid. Place the sorbet in the refrigerator for 10 minutes before serving. Scoop into serving dishes, decorate and serve.

Melon Ice ▶

VANILLA MOUSSE

Serves 4

This light and fluffy mousse tastes as good as it looks. It is served with a delicious raspberry sauce.

INGREDIENTS

For the mousse

300 ml/½ pt plain yoghurt

150 g/5 oz cream cheese

1 tsp vanilla essence

4 tbsp vanilla or caster sugar

1 tbsp brandy or sherry

2 tsp vegetarian gelatine

2 large egg whites

For the sauce

300 g/10 oz raspberries

Juice of 1 orange

50 g/2 oz icing sugar, sieved

Place the yoghurt, cheese, vanilla essence, sugar and brandy or sherry in a food processor, blend for 30 seconds until smooth. Pour into a mixing bowl.

Sprinkle the vegetarian gelatine onto 4 tablespoons of cold water in the saucepan. Stir until dissolved and heat to boiling point. Boil for 2 minutes.

Cool, then stir into the yoghurt mixture. Whisk the egg whites until soft peaks form and fold into the mousse.

Line a 900-ml/1½-pt loaf tin with clingfilm. Pour the mousse into the prepared tin and chill for 2 hours until set. Meanwhile, place the sauce ingredients in a food processor and blend until smooth. Push through a sieve to remove the seeds. Unmould the mousse onto a plate, remove the clingfilm, pour a little sauce onto a plate, slice the mousse and serve.

BANANA ICE CREAM

Serves 4

This is really a cheat's ice cream. Made with frozen bananas and plain yoghurt, the freezing time of the completed recipe is greatly reduced.

INGREDIENTS

250 g/8 oz bananas, chopped and frozen

1 tbsp lemon juice

6 tbsp icing sugar

150 ml/¼ pt plain yoghurt

Grated rind of 1 lemon

Small meringues, to serve (optional)

Set the freezer to rapid-freeze. Place the frozen bananas in a food processor with the lemon juice, sugar and yoghurt. Process for 1 minute or until smooth. Stir in the lemon rind.

Place the mixture in a freezerproof container, cover and freeze for 2 hours or until set. Scoop into dishes and serve with small meringues, if liked.

◄ *Vanilla Mousse*

BLUEBERRY CHEESECAKE

Serves 6

A cheesecake with a delicious granola and dried fig base.

INGREDIENTS

For the base	For the filling	For the topping
250 g/8 oz granola	1 tsp vegetarian gelatine	500 g/1 lb blueberries
150 g/5 oz dried figs	125 ml/4 fl oz skimmed evaporated milk	2 nectarines, pitted and sliced
	1 egg	2 tbsp clear honey
	6 tbsp caster sugar	
	500 g/1 lb cottage cheese	
	125 g/4 oz blueberries	

Place the granola and dried figs in a food processor and blend for 30 seconds. Press into the base of a base-lined 20-cm/8-in spring-release tin and chill while preparing the filling.

In a saucepan, sprinkle the gelatine onto 4 tablespoons of cold water. Stir until dissolved and heat to boiling point. Boil for 2 minutes, then cool.

Place the milk, egg, sugar and cheese in a food processor and blend until smooth. Stir in the blueberries. Place in a mixing bowl and gradually stir in the dissolved gelatine. Pour the mixture onto the base and chill for 2 hours until set.

Remove the cheesecake from the tin and arrange the fruit for the topping in alternate rings on top. Drizzle the honey over the fruit and serve.

CREME CARAMEL
Makes 4

INGREDIENTS

125 g/4 oz caster sugar plus 2 tsp extra
2 eggs, beaten
300 ml/¹/₂ pt skimmed milk
¹/₂ tsp vanilla essence
Pinch of ground cinnamon

Dissolve the sugar in a pan with 150 ml/¹/₄ pt cold water. Bring to the boil and boil rapidly until the mixture begins to turn golden brown. Pour into the base of four 150-ml/¹/₄-pt ramekin dishes.

Whisk the eggs with 2 tsp sugar in a bowl. Heat the milk with the vanilla essence and cinnamon until just boiling and gradually whisk into the egg mixture.

Pour into the ramekins and place in a shallow roasting tin with enough hot water to reach halfway up the sides. Cover and cook in the oven at 175°C/350°F/Gas 5 for 50 minutes until set. Remove from the tin, cool slightly and chill in the refrigerator for 1 hour. Unmould onto individual plates and serve immediately.

Blueberry Cheesecake ▶

PLUM AND GINGER BRULEE

Serves 4

Plums and ginger are a great combination in this easy brûlée recipe, the ginger adding just enough spice to complement the plums.

INGREDIENTS

4 plums, pitted and chopped

300 ml/½ pt single cream

250 ml/8 fl oz plain yoghurt

½ tsp ground ginger

4 tbsp granulated brown sugar

Spoon the plums into the base of four 150-ml/¼ pt ramekin dishes. Lightly whip the cream and fold in the yoghurt and ground ginger. Spoon onto the fruit and chill for 2 hours.

Sprinkle the brown sugar on top of the yoghurt mixture and grill for 5 minutes or until the sugar has dissolved. Chill for 20 minutes before serving

CAPPUCCINO SPONGE PUDDINGS

Serves 4

These individual sponge puddings are delicious served with coffee sauce. Ideal for dinner parties, they look more delicate and attractive than one large pudding.

INGREDIENTS

2 tbsp polyunsaturated margarine

2 tbsp granulated brown sugar

2 egg whites

50 g/2 oz plain flour

¾ tsp baking powder

6 tbsp skimmed milk

1 tsp coffee essence

½ tsp unsweetened cocoa powder

For the coffee sauce

300 ml/½ pt milk

1 tbsp granulated brown sugar

1 tsp coffee essence

1 tsp coffee liqueur (optional)

2 tbsp cornflour

Lightly grease four 150-ml/¼-pt individual pudding moulds. Cream the margarine and the sugar together in a bowl and add the egg whites. Sift the flour and baking powder together and fold into the creamed mixture with a metal spoon. Gradually stir in the milk, coffee essence and cocoa.

Spoon equal amounts of the mixture into the moulds. Cover with pleated wax paper, then foil, and tie securely with string. Place in a steamer or pan with sufficient boiling water to reach halfway up the sides of the moulds. Cover and

cook for 30 minutes or until cooked through.

Meanwhile, place the milk, sugar, coffee essence and coffee liqueur, if using, in a pan to make the sauce. Blend the cornflour with 4 tablespoons of cold water and stir into the pan. Bring to the boil, stirring until thickened. Reduce the heat and cook for a further 2 to 3 minutes.

Carefully remove the cooked puddings from the steamer. Remove the paper and foil and unmould onto individual plates. Spoon the sauce around and serve.

Plum and Ginger Brûlée ▶

FIG AND PEACH SOUFFLE

Serves 4

This is a delicately flavoured soufflé. The figs need to be ripe for the best results and the peaches not too large. Lime juice is the preferred choice, but lemon is a suitable substitute.

INGREDIENTS

250 g/8 oz ripe figs	150 ml/¼ pt whipping cream, lightly whipped
2 peaches	
125 g/4 oz plus 2 tbsp sugar	
50 ml/2 fl oz water	**To decorate**
3 eggs, separated	Cream, for piping
1 tbsp vegetarian gelatine, dissolved in	1 fig
5 tbsp hot water	Frosted geranium leaves (if available)
2 tbsp lime or lemon juice	

Tie a double band of wax paper around a 1-l/1¾-pt soufflé dish. The paper should stand 5 cm/2 in above the rim of the dish and be tight against the side. Lightly brush the inside with oil.

Remove the stems from the figs, wipe the fruit and cut each into four. Skin the peaches, pit and cut into four. In a pan, dissolve 50 g/2 oz sugar in the water, and put the fruit into the pan and cook very gently to just soften the fruit. Remove, cool and blend.

Place the egg yolks in a bowl with the remaining 2 tablespoons sugar over a pan of hot water and beat until light and fluffy. Remove the pan from the heat and continue beating until cool. Add the gelatine to the lime or lemon juice and fruit purée, and add this to the egg mixture with the whipped cream. Whisk the egg whites until stiff, fold into the fruit mixture and pour into the prepared soufflé dish. Put into a cool place until set.

Carefully remove the collar from the soufflé. Pipe cream around the top edge and decorate with thin fig slices and geranium leaves (if available).

ICED BLACKCURRANT SOUFFLE

Serves 6

Fresh blackcurrants are available in the summer months. Always select plump juicy fruit.

INGREDIENTS

750 g/1½ lb blackcurrants, hulled

175 g/6 oz sugar

2 egg whites

125 g/4 oz icing sugar, sifted

300 ml/½ pt whipping cream

Wrap a double thickness of foil around a 1-l/1¾-pt soufflé dish to extend 5 cm/2 in above the rim of the dish. Cook the blackcurrants with the sugar until soft, purée in a blender or food processor then sieve. Leave to cool. Whisk the egg whites until stiff, then gradually whisk in the icing sugar.

Whip the cream until softly stiff. Place the fruit purée in a large bowl and gradually fold in the egg white and cream. Pour into the prepared soufflé dish, level the surface and freeze for several hours until solid. Remove the foil and serve.

SURPRISE BANANA PUFFS

Makes approximately 20 puffs

A delicious fruit-filled variation on profiteroles.

INGREDIENTS

500 g/1 lb ripe bananas

Juice of 1 orange

90 g/3 oz soft brown sugar

250 ml/8 fl oz Greek yoghurt

For the choux pastry

60 g/2 oz butter or margarine

125 ml/4 fl oz water

50 g/2 oz plus 2 tbsp plain flour

2 eggs

For the caramel sauce

250 ml/8 fl oz sugar

8 tbsp water

Peel and mash the bananas in a bowl with the orange juice and sugar. Whisk in the yoghurt, pour into a suitable container and freeze, beating three times at regular intervals.

Place the butter or margarine in a medium-sized saucepan and pour in the water. Heat gently until the fat melts, then turn the heat up and bring to a full boil. Tip in all the flour, remove the pan from the heat and mix until smooth, when the mixture should come away from the sides of the pan. Leave to cool.

Preheat the oven to 220°C/425°F/Gas 7. Grease two baking sheets. Have ready a large piping bag fitted with a large fluted nozzle.

Beat the eggs and gradually beat into the lukewarm mixture in the pan. Continue beating until the mixture is smooth and glossy. Fill the pastry bag with the mixture and pipe small mounds onto the greased baking sheets, leaving enough space between for the puffs to expand. Bake for 10 minutes, then reduce the oven temperature to 190°C/375°F/Gas 5 and cook for a further 10 minutes. Remove from the oven. Slit with a sharp knife and cool on a wire rack.

Make the sauce by placing the sugar and remaining water in a saucepan. Heat gently to dissolve the sugar. When dissolved, bring to the boil and cook until it begins to change colour. When the syrup becomes a golden colour, cover your hand with a teatowel, lift the pan from the heat and quickly dip the base in cold water to stop the caramel overcooking. Add a little boiling water to the pan for a runny caramel for pouring over the puffs. Keep on one side.

Place the ice cream in the refrigerator for 30 minutes before filling the puffs. Serve with the caramel sauce.

GRAPE CUSTARDS

Serves 4

This delightful dessert is quick and simple to make. It is ideal for a dinner party.

INGREDIENTS

250 g/8 oz seedless red grapes

4 egg yolks

3 tbsp caster sugar

4 tbsp Marsala, Madeira or sweet sherry

Wash the grapes and place in the bottom of four individual glasses.

Place the egg yolks in a bowl. Beat lightly, add the sugar and wine and mix together. Place the bowl over a pan of hot water and whisk until the mixture is thick and creamy. This could take about 10 minutes.

Divide the mixture among the glasses and serve at once while still warm with sponge fingers.

ORANGE AND STRAWBERRY SYLLABUB

Serves 6

A tasty fruit version of a syllabub. The fruits may be varied, depending on the time of year.

INGREDIENTS

300 g/10 oz fresh strawberries

Juice and coarsely grated peel of 1 orange

1 tbsp Grand Marnier or Cointreau

3 tbsp caster sugar

90 ml/3 fl oz white wine

1 tsp lemon juice

300 ml/½ pt double cream

2 egg whites

Wash and hull the strawberries. Slice and arrange in the bottom of six sundae glasses. Sprinkle the orange juice and the liqueur over the strawberries.

Place the caster sugar, wine and lemon juice in a mixing bowl. Add half the grated orange peel together with the cream and stir until the ingredients are absorbed by the cream.

Whisk the egg whites until stiff. Add to the cream and continue whisking until the mixture is softly stiff. Spoon on top of the strawberries and sprinkle with the remaining orange peel. Serve well chilled.

GOLDEN SUMMER PUDDING

Serves 6

This is a variation on the traditional summer pudding.

INGREDIENTS

2 oranges

500 ml/1 pt water

6 tbsp granulated sugar

2 peaches or nectarines

2 mangoes

12 slices white bread

To decorate

Mango slices (optional)

Orange slices (optional)

Remove the peel from the oranges and place the peel in a saucepan with the water and sugar. Dissolve the sugar and cook gently for 2 minutes to extract the flavour from the orange peel. Remove the pan from the heat and discard the orange peel.

Skin the peaches or nectarines and mangoes, and remove the stones. Cut the flesh into small dice, add to the flavoured syrup and cook to just soften the fruit, about 5 minutes. Remove from the heat.

Cut 12 rounds of bread to fit the base and tops of six 150-ml/¹/₄-pt ramekin dishes and place a round in the base of each dish. Cut small squares of bread and use to line the sides of the dishes.

Using a slotted spoon, fill each dish with the fruit, reserving the syrup to serve with the puddings. Top each with the remaining circles of bread, pressing down well. Cover each tightly with clingfilm and leave to chill overnight.

To serve, remove carefully from the dishes, spoon the remaining syrup over, and decorate, if liked, with extra slices of mango or orange.

173

CAKES, BAKES AND COOKIES

RAISIN AND HONEY BREAD

Serves 16

This loaf contains a high proportion of yoghurt which gives it a white, light centre.
Serve with butter and jam for a tasty afternoon treat.

INGREDIENTS

260 g/9 oz plain flour

1½ tsp baking powder

½ tsp bicarbonate of soda

½ tsp salt

400 ml/14 fl oz plain yoghurt

2 egg whites

90 g/3 oz raisins

2 tbsp clear honey

Polyunsaturated margarine, for greasing

Mix the flour, baking powder, bicarbonate of soda and salt in a large bowl. Whisk together the yoghurt and egg whites, and fold into the flour mixture with the raisins and honey.

Grease a 1-kg/2-lb loaf pan and spoon in the mixture. Bake in the oven at 200°C/425°F/Gas 6 for 20 minutes until golden. Cool slightly and turn out of the pan. Serve warm.

OAT AND ORANGE BISCUITS

Makes 20

*These little biscuits are hard to resist. Rolled in oatmeal, they have a crunchy
outside, and softer inside which has a mild orange flavour.*

INGREDIENTS

3 tbsp polyunsaturated margarine

50 g/2 oz granulated brown sugar

1 egg white, lightly beaten

2 tbsp skimmed milk

3 tbsp raisins

Grated rind of 1 orange

150 g/5 oz self-raising flour

90 g/3 oz oatmeal

Strips of orange rind, to decorate

(optional)

Cream the margarine and sugar together until light and fluffy. Add the egg white, milk, raisins and orange rind. Fold in the flour and bring the mixture together to form a dough. Roll into 20 equal-sized balls.

Place the oatmeal in a shallow bowl, roll each dough ball in the oatmeal to coat completely, pressing them on gently. Place the biscuits on non-stick baking sheets, spacing well apart. Flatten each round slightly.

Bake at 175°C/350°F/Gas 4 for 15 minutes or until golden. Cool on a wire rack, decorate and store any leftovers in an airtight container.

GINGERBREAD

Makes 16 portions

INGREDIENTS

480 g/1 lb plain flour

Pinch of salt

1 tbsp ground ginger

1 tbsp baking powder

1 tsp bicarbonate of soda

250 g/8 oz granulated brown sugar

125 g/4 oz molasses

125 g/4 oz syrup

150 g/5 oz dried pitted prunes

300 ml/½ pt skimmed milk

1 egg white

Icing sugar, for dusting

2 pieces preserved stem ginger, chopped

Grease and line a 22-cm/9-in square tin. Sift the flour, salt, ground ginger, baking powder and bicarbonate into a large bowl.

Place the sugar, molasses and syrup in a pan and heat gently to dissolve. Place the dried prunes in a food processor with 3 tablespoons of water and blend for 30 seconds until puréed. Add the milk to the sugar mixture and stir into the dry ingredients with the prunes, mixing well. Whisk the egg white until peaks form, fold into the mixture and spoon into the prepared tin.

Bake at 175°C/350°F/Gas 4 for 55 minutes or until firm. Cool in the tin for 10 minutes. Turn the cake out onto a wire rack and cool completely. Cut into 16 pieces. Dust with icing sugar and top with chopped stem ginger.

CHOCOLATE BROWNIES

Makes 16

These chocolate brownies are low-fat – they taste just as good as the real thing but have a slightly different texture. Keep in an airtight container if you can resist them for long enough.

INGREDIENTS

150 g/5 oz pitted dried prunes

175 g/6 oz granulated brown sugar

3 tbsp unsweetened cocoa powder, sifted

50 g/2 oz flour

1 tsp baking powder

3 egg whites

Icing sugar, for dusting

Lightly grease and line a shallow 18-cm/7-in square cake tin.

Place the prunes in a food processor with 3 tablespoons of water and blend to a purée. Transfer the purée to a mixing bowl and stir in the sugar, cocoa, flour and baking powder. Whisk the egg whites until peaks form and fold into the mixture. Pour into the prepared tin and level the surface.

Bake at 175°C/350°F/Gas 4 for 1 hour or until cooked through. Let the brownies cool in the tin for 10 minutes, then turn out onto a wire rack and cool completely. Cut into 16 squares, dust with icing sugar and serve.

Gingerbread ▶

PEAR UPSIDE-DOWN CAKE

Makes 8 slices

In this recipe, sliced pears are set on a caramel base and topped with a spicy sponge mixture. Once cooked, turn out and serve immediately with plain yoghurt.

INGREDIENTS

2 tbsp clear honey

2 tbsp granulated brown sugar

2 large pears, peeled, cored and sliced

4 tbsp polyunsaturated margarine

50 g/2 oz fine granulated sugar

3 egg whites

125 g/4 oz self-raising flour

2 tsp ground allspice

Walnuts to decorate (optional)

Heat the honey and sugar in a pan until melted. Pour into a base-lined 20-cm/8-in round cake tin. Arrange the pears around the base of the tin.

Cream the margarine and sugar together until light and fluffy. Whisk the egg whites until peaks form and fold into the mixture with the flour and allspice.

Spoon on top of the pears.

Bake at 175°C/350°F/Gas 4 for 50 minutes or until risen. Leave in the tin for 5 minutes, then turn out onto a serving plate. Remove the lining paper, decorate with walnuts, and serve.

FRUIT AND NUT LOAF

Makes 12 slices

This is a sweet, fruity bread rather than a teabread. Slice and serve with butter.

INGREDIENTS

250 g/8 oz strong white flour

½ tsp salt

1 tbsp polyunsaturated margarine

1 tbsp fine granulated sugar

150 g/5 oz raisins

50 g/2 oz walnuts, chopped

2 tsp active dry yeast

5 tbsp skimmed milk

1 tbsp clear honey

Sift the flour and salt into a bowl. Rub in the margarine, then stir in the sugar, raisins, walnuts and yeast. Pour the milk in a pan with 5 tablespoons of water. Heat gently until lukewarm, but do not boil. Add the lukewarm liquid to the dry ingredients in the bowl and bring the mixture together to form a dough.

Turn the dough onto a lightly floured surface and knead for 5 to 7 minutes until smooth and elastic. Shape the dough into a round and place on a non-stick baking sheet. Make parallel diagonal slits across the top of the loaf, working from left to right. Then turn the knife and work back towards you making parallel diagonal slits to form "diamond" shapes. Cover and leave to rise in a warm place for 1 hour or until doubled in size.

Bake at 220°C/425°F/Gas 7 for 35 minutes or until cooked through. Place on a wire rack and brush with honey. Cool and serve.

Pear Upside-Down Cake ▶

APPLE BRAN CAKE

Makes 12 slices

Chunks of apple add moisture to this filling cake. Decorate with apple slices just before serving or brush with a little lemon juice if you wish to store the cake.

INGREDIENTS

125 ml/4 fl oz plus 2 tbsp apple sauce

125 g/4 oz plus 2 tbsp brown sugar

3 tbsp skimmed milk

175 g/6 oz flour

15 g/1 oz All-bran cereal

2 tsp baking powder

1 tsp ground cinnamon

2 tbsp clear honey

150 g/5 oz apples, peeled and chopped

2 egg whites

Apple slices and 1 tbsp honey, to decorate

Lightly grease and base line a deep 20-cm/8-in round cake tin.

Place the apple sauce in a mixing bowl with the sugar and milk. Sift the flour into the bowl and add the bran, baking powder, cinnamon, honey and apples. Whisk the egg whites until peaks form and fold into the mixture. Spoon the mixture into the prepared tin and level the surface.

Bake at 160°C/350°F/Gas 4 for 1¼–1½ hours or until cooked through. Cool in the tin for 10 minutes, then turn onto a wire rack and cool completely. Arrange the apple slices on top and drizzle with honey.

Apple Bran Cake ▶

SEED BREAD

Serves 12

INGREDIENTS

1 sachet active dry yeast

480 g/1 lb wholemeal flour

2 tsp granulated sugar

2 tsp salt

2 tbsp polyunsaturated margarine

2 tsp caraway seeds

2 tsp fennel seeds

2 tsp sesame seeds

1 egg white

Place the yeast, flour, sugar and salt in a bowl. Rub in the margarine and add half of each of the seeds. Stir in 300 ml/ ½ pt lukewarm water and mix well. Bring the mixture together to form a soft dough. Knead for 5 minutes on a floured surface and break into six pieces.

Lightly grease a deep 15-cm/6-in round cake tin. Shape each of the dough pieces into a round. Place five pieces around the edge of the pan and one in the centre.

Cover and leave to prove in a warm place for 1 hour or until doubled in size.

Whisk the egg white and brush over the top of the dough. Sprinkle the remaining seeds over the top of the dough, alternating the different types on each section of the loaf.

Bake at 200˚C/400°F/Gas 6 for 30 minutes or until cooked through. The loaf should sound hollow when tapped on the base. Cool slightly and serve.

HERBED CHEESE LOAF

Serves 8

This loaf is best served straight from the oven to obtain the full flavour of the herbs and cheese.

INGREDIENTS

1 sachet active dry yeast

750 g/1½ lb strong white flour

1 tsp salt

1 tsp fine granulated sugar

1 tbsp polyunsaturated margarine

3 tbsp chopped fresh parsley

175 g/6 oz grated low-fat cheese

1 egg white

Place the yeast, flour, salt and sugar in a large mixing bowl. Rub in the margarine. Add the herbs and cheese and stir in 500 ml/1 pt lukewarm water. Bring together to form a soft dough. Knead on a lightly floured surface for 5 to 7 minutes until smooth.

Divide the mixture into three equal portions. Roll each into a 35-cm/14-in sausage shape. Place the dough pieces side by side and cross them over each other at the top, pressing together to seal.

Continue working down the length of the dough, crossing alternate strands to form a plait. Seal the end by pressing together and fold both ends under the plait.

Place the bread on a non-stick baking sheet, cover and leave in a warm place for 1 hour or until doubled in size. Lightly beat the egg white and brush over the loaf. Bake at 200˚C/400°F/Gas 6 for 30 minutes or until cooked through. The loaf should sound hollow when tapped on the base. Serve.

◀ *Seed Bread*

WHOLEMEAL SODA BREAD

Makes 12 slices

This yeast-free bread is based on a traditional Irish recipe. Made with wholemeal flour
for extra goodness, it is filling and ideal served with soup.

INGREDIENTS

175 g/6 oz plain flour

175 g/6 oz wholemeal flour

2 tsp bicarbonate of soda

2 tsp cream of tartar

$^1/_2$ tsp salt

2 tbsp polyunsaturated margarine

375 ml/12 fl oz skimmed milk

2 egg whites, beaten

Lightly grease and flour a baking sheet. Sieve the flours, bicarbonate of soda, cream of tartar and salt into a bowl. Add the contents of the sieve to the bowl.

Rub in the margarine and gradually mix in the milk and beaten egg whites to form a dough. Shape the mixture into a round on a lightly floured surface. Score into four triangles with a knife and place on the prepared baking sheet. Bake at 220˚C/425°F/Gas 7 for 30 minutes or until cooked. Serve warm.

CONTINENTAL PLUM CAKE

Serves 6

This is a deliciously light sponge with a difference. For best results the eggs should be weighed and the sugar, butter and flour should each be the same weight as the eggs.

INGREDIENTS

175 g/6 oz caster sugar

175 g/6 oz butter, melted and cooled

½ tsp vanilla essence

3 eggs, separated

175 g/6 oz self-raising flour, sifted

375 g/12 oz firm, small plums, pitted and halved

Icing sugar, for dredging

Preheat the oven to 200°C/400°F/Gas 6. Line the base of a 18 x 25-cm/7½ x 10-in roasting tin with baking parchment.

Beat the caster sugar and melted butter until light and fluffy. Add the vanilla essence and beat in one egg yolk at a time. If it curdles, add a little flour.

Whisk the egg whites until stiff and gradually fold into the creamed mixture alternately with the flour. Spoon into the prepared tin, level the surface and arrange the plums over the top.

Bake for about 40 to 45 minutes until risen and golden and no mark is left when you press it lightly with your fingertips. Allow to cool slightly before removing from the tin and peel off the parchment if serving hot. Sprinkle with icing sugar and serve either hot or cold.

APRICOT BARS

Makes 8

These are very filling, healthy fruit bars. A delicious apricot purée is sandwiched between a shortcake mixture.

INGREDIENTS

175 g/6 oz dried apricots, chopped

4 tbsp unsweetened orange juice

6 tbsp polyunsaturated margarine, melted

4 tbsp clear honey

50 g/2 oz semolina flour

125 g/4 oz plus 2 tbsp plain flour

Lightly grease an 18-cm/7-in square cake tin. Place the apricots in a pan with the orange juice and simmer for 5 minutes. Drain if the juice has not been absorbed by the fruit.

Heat the margarine and honey in a pan until melted. Add the semolina and flour and mix well. Press half of the semolina mixture into the base of the prepared tin. Spoon on the fruit mixture and top with the remaining semolina mix, covering the fruit completely.

Bake at 200°C/400°F/Gas 6 for 35 minutes until risen and golden brown. Cool for 5 minutes in the tin, then cut into eight bars. Remove from the tin to a wire rack, leave to cool completely, and then serve.

LOW-FAT CHOCOLATE CAKE

Makes 12 slices

This chocolate cake is very rich and a small slice will satisfy any chocoholic for a while.

INGREDIENTS

50 g/2 oz polyunsaturated margarine

300 g/10 oz granulated brown sugar

2 egg whites

150 g/5 oz plain flour

3 tbsp unsweetened cocoa powder, sifted

1/4 tsp bicarbonate of soda

1/4 tsp baking powder

250 ml/8 fl oz skimmed milk

Icing sugar and cocoa,

for dusting

Grease and flour a 20-cm/8-in round cake tin. Cream the margarine and sugar in a bowl until light and fluffy. Add the egg whites and whisk into the mixture until thick.

Place the flour, cocoa, bicarbonate of soda and baking powder in a separate bowl. Add the milk gradually to the egg white mixture, alternating with the dry ingredients. Pour the mixture into the prepared tin.

Bake in the oven at 200°C/400°F/Gas 6 for 1 hour or until cooked through. Leave to cool completely in the tin. Turn out and dust with the icing sugar and cocoa. Serve immediately.

Apricot Bars ▶

CARROT AND PRUNE CAKE

Makes 12 slices

The carrot and prunes make this a gloriously moist cake.

Take extra care folding in the egg whites as a heavy hand will result in a heavy cake.

INGREDIENTS

250 g/8 oz carrots	**For the icing**
1 400-g/14-oz can prunes in fruit juice	175 g/6 oz soft cheese
300 g/10 oz granulated brown sugar	1 tbsp icing sugar, sieved
300 g/10 oz self-raising flour	Ground cinnamon and orange rind,
Grated rind of 1 orange	to decorate
3 tbsp semolina flour	
3 egg whites	

Grease and base line a 20-cm/8-in deep cake tin. Grate the carrots and place in a bowl. Drain the prunes and discard the juice and pits. Blend the prunes in a food processor for 30 seconds and add to the carrot with the sugar. Add the flour, orange rind, reserving a little to decorate, and semolina to the mixture, stirring well. Whisk the egg whites until peaks form and fold into the mixture. Spoon into the prepared tin and level the surface.

Bake at 200°C/400°F/Gas 6 for 45 minutes or until cooked through. Cool in the tin for 10 minutes, turn out and cool completely on a wire rack.

Mix together the cream cheese and icing sugar for the icing. Spread on top of the cake. Decorate and serve.

INDEX